on pages 105

Other similar books by Stan Johnson:

J'Ever Notice?
2003

'Zat Right?
2007

Editor: Frances Johnson
Photographer: Stan Johnson

Y'Reckon?

Stan Johnson

authorHOUSE®

AuthorHouse™
1663 Liberty Drive
Bloomington, IN 47403
www.authorhouse.com
Phone: 1-800-839-8640

First published by AuthorHouse   7/6/2010

ISBN: 978-1-4520-1792-1 (e)
ISBN: 978-1-4520-1790-7 (sc)
ISBN: 978-1-4520-1791-4 (hc)

Library of Congress Control Number: 2010905940

Printed in the United States of America
Bloomington, Indiana

This book is printed on acid-free paper.

For information write to:

Stan Johnson
PO Box 444
Sweetwater, Texas 79556

Unless otherwise noted, all people, places and stories in this book are as real as a full moon coming up on a clear night. If you think you recognize a person or place in these stories, you probably do.

Contents

Page 105 on Don Abb. (handwritten annotation)

Country Stories

One Hundred Years Ago

MY DADDY, CLAUDE Freeman Johnson, was born on August 11. Oh, yeah, I almost forgot to say it was one hundred years ago, but I guess my story title gave that away, didn't it? He was born on a farm east of Sylvester. He was the third child in the family, and also the third son. One of his brothers had been born in 1900 and the other in 1902. His mother and daddy were born in November of 1882, which would make them both twenty-two when Daddy came along. They had been married six years.

Let's look at this for a while and think about it. In 1905, Sylvester was actually a town with a bank, school, stores, and everything, including a train that came through. But out on a farm, things were a lot different than they would be today. There was of course a farmhouse, probably of the box-and-strip construction that's so popular for the inside of some steak or barbecue places today. That means vertical 1 x 12 lumber stands side by side with 1 x 4's nailed over the cracks from the outside. This was the wall of a house, inside and outside, and there would be wood floors, a front and back door, a few windows, and a cedar-shingle roof. A cistern that caught water off the roof into gutters when it rained. No water in the house except what came up on the end of a rope in a bucket and was carried in. Kerosene lamps for light, a wood-burning stove for cooking and heat. A kitchen, dining room, living room and maybe two bedrooms. A front porch and maybe a back porch, an outhouse, barn, lots, and a storm cellar. If the family had been there awhile, they might have a chicken house and pigpen, or these might have been part of the barn.

On the day Daddy was born, Papa Johnson was probably there alone with Mama Johnson. Maybe the three and five-year-old boys were playing outside. Really think now—not about what was there, but about what was not there. No running water, no central heat and central air, no electric power, no phone, no car, no ambulance, no 911, no Rolling Plains Hospital, no medicine and no Dr. Glover. And we think we've felt alone and apprehensive? I know this was the third one, but still! Mama and Papa Johnson went on to have seven boys and three girls, and they all lived to grow up. The first one to die was Daddy's brother Arthur, born in 1907, who lived until 1943.

Just think about Mama Johnson having Daddy in August. It was hot, you know it was, and maybe dry too. She would have to have been worn out and weak. And think about Papa Johnson on that farm. A wife in bed with a new baby, a three-year-old and a five-year-old on the loose, a cotton crop, maize crop, garden, cows to milk, horses to feed, washing and cooking to do, wood to cut, water to draw and on and on and on. How in the wide world did they do it? But they all did!

I stop and think that a while back we were having trouble with our Internet provider, my cell phone didn't work but about half the time, and on top of all that Frances's car was in the shop for a few days and we had to share my pickup. We considered this an inconvenience that was really, really trying! I guess we 'ort' to be ashamed. Y'reckon?

The Gin

KIDS TODAY PROBABLY wouldn't know how exciting a trip to the cotton gin was back when. Y'reckon? Yeah, I do. They don't have any way to know. Let me set a stage so you will kinda see how it was for us in the country, and what made that trip such a treat for us kids.

First of all, when someone was going to build a house, they usually went out in the edge of the pasture and cut down a few mesquite trees and then grubbed up the stumps. Real hard work before they even started to work. They would likely build a 24 x 30 foundation, which as you can see, makes a 720-square-foot house. Some houses lately have a "great room" that large or larger! Or maybe they would lay out a 30 x 30 plan so they could have a big 900-square-foot house. It would be a frame house with cedar shingles, two front doors for ventilation, and windows. The floor plan would consist of four rooms of about equal size. There might be one small room they called the "bathroom", but there was no running water. Some of the windows might have screens, at least the ones on the north and south sides of the house, so the southwest breeze could blow through the rooms.

Outside, it was necessary to dig a hole off one corner of the house for a cistern to catch water. There would be gutters around the roof edge to catch rainwater and pour it off into the cistern. The ones doing the building would take a team with a wagon and barrel or a slide and barrel to someone's tank. The barrel was filled up with tank water, probably muddy, and taken back to be poured into the cistern to last until it rained and the cistern caught rainwater. Of course, this might have to be repeated several times in order to have enough water to start with.

These houses had beds, a sparse amount of other furniture and maybe an icebox to put blocks of ice in. There was no electricity, running water or telephone. There might be a battery-operated radio that could be used only sparingly because the battery would run down. It would be unlikely to see any books, magazines or newspapers lying around the way they are now. There probably was a drugstore calendar, a Sears and Roebuck catalogue and a Bible.

Now, finally, I said all that to say that something like the cotton gin might as well have been the Houston Space Center, the circus and Six Flags all rolled into one. Imagine a giant building with lights, machinery and men working around the clock. The gin had an office with a big window so the people inside could see who was bringing cotton. Outside were the drive-on scales where a wagonload of cotton could be weighed. Once in a while most of the kids got to go to the gin. I would go with Uncle Herbert, and he would be pulling the wagon that Granddaddy Rudd had brought when he came from Comanche County to Palava in 1906. I would get to sit on the square axle housing beside the tractor seat. Part of the excitement of the trip was visiting the store in Palava. They had peanuts in a little cardboard container kinda like a Garrett snuff can and Barq's Root Beer. We always envied the kids who lived in or near town (Palava) because they could be at the gin anytime they wanted to. They got to hang around all the farmers who had brought cotton in, and hear all the news and cussing and everything. The big galvanized pipe that sucked the cotton up was awesome. We heard many tales of hats, caps and maybe even one kid lost up the suction. The gin at Palava, it really was truly awesome to a small country boy.

Most of the cotton was brought in to the gin with tractors pulling wagons or trailers, but I faintly remember a few horse or mule teams bringing it. Farmers then usually had a tractor, and a car that they used to go to town and to church. There were very few pickups, and probably as many one and two-ton trucks. Farmers caught their own cotton seed at the gin and if they needed sudan, hegari or gooseneck maize seed they could get a sack of it at the feed store in town and put it in the trunk of their car.

Palava One Hundred Years Ago

LEE AND ADA Rudd, my maternal grandparents, moved with their five children from Comanche County to Palava one hundred years ago this month. Y'reckon? Yeah, I do. It was in January of 1906. They bought a hundred and sixty acres about a mile and a half east of Palava, on the south side of the Palava Road in the corner at the crossroads and east of the Eskota-Longworth highway. They paid a dollar and fifty cents an acre for it, and Granddaddy Rudd thought he'd be in debt forever! Mama said there was a little house down close to a draw in the middle of the place. Seems as if they stayed there and in the wagons at first, but I imagine that after traveling in wagons for a week with five children from two to eight years old and camping along the way every night, any house at all would have looked good to them. First of all, they built a house in the middle of the west side of the place close to the Eskota Road. Then they built a barn to go with the pens they'd already built, dug and plastered two cisterns, dug a storm cellar and built a smoke house. They dug a tank and built a dam east of the house pretty close to the barn. Mama was born in the fall of that year, and was the sixth child of eight.

The Rudds were just one family of several that had moved to Palava. A few years ago I set out to gather information about the families who'd been there the longest. At our reunion, I put a notebook by the sign-in sheet and asked everyone to fill in what they knew about their own families, along with the year they had settled out there. This is what I learned. In 1874, Charles Byrd, a Texas Ranger, came to Palava. This was even before Fisher County had been established. He opened the first store, the first cotton gin, and the first post office. Then sixteen years before Granddaddy and Grandmother Rudd came, the Godfreys moved in from Ellis County in 1890. They lived east of Palava and south of the road. Luther Howard, the Godfreys' grandson, came with them from Ellis County and brought his wife who was from Hope, Arkansas. Then in 1895, Julian Moody and his family came from Vernon and moved in southwest of Palava. The original Moody School was named for them, and was southwest of the Rock Creek Bridge. The cistern is still there, but the school itself was later moved to one mile west of Highway 70 at the Palava turnoff.

In 1889, W.T. Harvey, father of Bill Harvey, had run off from his home in Llano when he was eleven years old to join a cattle drive. The cattle were driven through the Palava area. W.T. always remembered Fisher County and talked so much about it after he got back home from the drive that the whole family finally moved there in 1898.

W.D. Williams and his family came in south of Palava in 1898 from Ellis County. Stephen Jasper Nolan, Theta Kearney's daddy, came from Comanche County the same year and settled northwest of Palava. About that same time, J.A. Hall settled two miles east of Palava. He also came from Comanche County, and he paid a dollar and seventy-five cents an acre for his farm. The cistern is still there at his house place. Clifton Jay came from East Texas in 1900 and settled two miles southeast of Palava. John Jesse, father of Billie Diddle, came from St. Louis about that time, and L.L. Neeper came from Arkansas to settle two miles west of Palava. Joe Smith also came in 1903 from Arkansas and bought a farm a mile and a half east of Palava on the north side of the road. And along about that time the Kearneys moved on the farm right west of Palava and south of the road, and west of them is where the DeBusk family moved when they came from Hunt County.

Joel Houston Shedd brought his family from Georgetown and camped on a creek up by Hamlin before moving to Palava. Floy Hoover once told me her daddy, George Washington Hoover, came to Palava to visit W.D. Williams in 1900, and then in 1906, he decided to move his family there. They left Wood County and finally made it to the train in Fort Worth. They rode the train to Eskota, then walked seven miles to Palava. It had snowed seven inches. And guess what? It was New Year's Day in 1907 when they moved across the road west from the Rudd Family. I was a pallbearer at the funerals of both Floy and Jewel Hoover, and I couldn't help thinking, "They walked seven miles from Eskota to Palava in seven inches of snow on New Year's Day in 1907. I guess they came to stay." Now they're both at the Palava Cemetery.

All this happened a hundred years ago, and there were a lot more people living around Palava then than there are now.

· ·

P. S. A story that was told often among these early Palava people concerned one of their number who decided late in life to take a wife. Wanting to look his best for the occasion, he borrowed a suit and a pair of boots, then saw how nice he looked and went back to the owner to ask whether he might also borrow his false teeth.

Times Past

MOST TIMES WHEN you walk around an old house or barn you notice things that remind you of other things or make your imagination run rampant. Y'Reckon? Yeah, I really do. The other day at our farm I was throwing feed sacks into a cistern at a house that we've always called the Howard house. It was built in 1923 by Mr. Justiss, but Luther Howard and his family lived in it for a few years and that's where it got its name. One of Mr. Howard's girls, Guan, told me in 1985 that there had once been an old two-story house there that had been torn down to make a place for the new house. She said she had a picture of the first house somewhere and would show it to me if she could find it. I never did get to see it, though. Guan and her husband moved to California shortly after that, and later she died there. I can imagine a situation where Guan's children are going through all of her pictures after she died. I see them passing pictures around and asking if anyone has any idea of whose house this was or where it is. Everyone shakes their head and says something that means they have no idea, and the last one to look at the picture throws it in the trash. But really, what else is left to do? These people are living several states away and are all the family that's left.

Of course, in most cases like the one I've described, there's someone somewhere who would love to have the picture and might even have it enlarged and framed. I've had antique dealers tell me some people would actually buy those old oval-framed pictures, one of a man and one of a woman, hang them up at their home, and claim they were pictures of their great grandparents. I guess actually it's harmless enough. So many people really don't know anything about their family history, or maybe it's a case where Granny's house burned and all the pictures and the family Bible with birth, marriage and death records in it were destroyed.

On the other hand, a lot of people in this part of the country really do know quite a bit of history about their families on both sides. Of course, in keeping with human nature, most of these stories are flattering, good and honorable. A wise old straight-shooting fellow one time said, "If you really do want to know about your family back then, ask their neighbors."

After my cousin Buck Rudd died, we all sat around the kitchen table and looked through so many pictures that he had, some from our grandparents. We had a great sack of them with no names, no dates, and no clue to who the people in them were. We asked distant cousins and some people of the community to look through the "unknown" pile and identify some of them. But so many remain unknown. On the lighter side, as they say, Frances knows about a family picture that has been carefully identified. It shows several people and on the back side it says, "All of us at Mama's last Sunday."

....

P. S. Back in the fifties, two old men (no, I didn't just think so then) got into a scrap out at Starrs' Drive-in. The law was there pretty close by and jumped in and pulled them apart. One of the old men kept hollering, "This ain't fair, it just ain't fair!" Finally, one of the officers asked, "Well, why isn't it fair?" And the old man said, "That so and so bit me, and I didn't even have in my teeth!"

Hard Times Past, For Now

AGAIN, WHILE I was at the Howard House, I noticed something that seemed like signs of hard times. Y'reckon? Yeah, I really do. I noticed part of an old ruined back tractor tire that was probably left from a time close on either side of 1950. When I saw it, I thought, "That's a sign of hard times past." I know that if we ruin a back tractor tire now, it's fairly sickening to think that it will be six hundred or more dollars gone, plus lost time. I thought about the fact that replacing this ruined tire probably caused a lot of grief. Someone, or more than one, had to do without something they wanted and very likely needed. Was it the woman of the house, who had counted on a new Easter dress, or more likely the material, pattern, thread and buttons to make one? Or, was it in the fall and the children were looking forward to school clothes and supplies? Or, maybe the man needed to have his boots half soled? Who knows? I don't know, but we can safely bet that one or all of the family was more than mildly inconvenienced by this ruined tire that probably cost fifty dollars.

This set me to thinking about "back in then," as the kids say now. This was during the big dry which we are all so familiar with and that we do know can definitely be counted on. Which makes me wonder---why do some of us try to predict the rains and even offer to bet on them? I know, I know, "Fools and newcomers," and all that. I predicted one time when I thought it would rain and this wise guy said, "How long you lived around here?" I told him I'd been here all but ten years of my life up until that time, and he said, "Well, you're not a newcomer, so that don't leave but one thing." Why don't we just take the safer route and predict and bet on when it's going to be dry? I don't guess we could find anyone to bet with us.

Anyway, I had a long and solemn review of past dry spells. What I had seen and what I had heard about hard, dry times that came before. There was a big wet in the early Thirties with fat cattle and good cotton and feed crops, but it was during a devastating market wreck. After that came a big dry that resulted in lost land, homes, cattle and equity. This caused mental scars that some of the elderly still have and a lot have been buried with. My generation didn't live through that time, but a lot of us have repercussions from living with parents who did. I know I do. I can't waste anything or throw away much, and I still believe we will see the United States of America eventually suffer because of waste.

Hard Doings

BACK DURING THE years I've been writing about were some real hard times that I've always wanted to write about, but really wanted some sort of lead-in. Y'reckon? Yeah, I do, so I'm going to leave the stage set with the previous two stories.

In the Fifties, church, and especially going to church, was a big part of life. Then, as now and in hard times past, the rougher things got the better church attendance was. I was nine years old when the big dry of the Fifties started. One Sunday when I was eleven, this couple who lived in the Palava community wanted me to go home with them after church that morning and said they'd bring me back to church that night. They were a real nice religious couple who had never had any children. They were really devout and stayed in The Book all the time, and they loved to sing and pray. They never missed church. He always wore starched and ironed, new-looking bib overalls, a blue chambray shirt and those black, real shiny shoes that tied. Please, please understand, he did not dress like that because he thought it was smart, cute, "in", or because he just wanted to be comfortable. He, like all the rest of us, had been raised to wear the best he had to church, and that was the best he had. Anyway, I went home with them that day, and none of the following circumstances made a bit of difference to me at all. They lived in a house where a man, woman, eight children and a couple of cousins had lived before. I mean, it was a big house! They didn't anywhere near fill it up. I guarantee I could haul off all the furniture and possessions in that entire house in one crew-cab pickup. We sat around and read out of The Book, and talked about songs, crops and times past. Oh! You may wonder what we had for Sunday dinner....Post Toasties. It was all fine, and was a sign of the times. That was all they had to offer.

I can remember other people in those days who would get on hard times, and maybe their old car might quit on them so that they didn't have any way to get to town and buy groceries. Some neighbor would take them if they didn't have any family to ride with. The most awful thing would be if some of them got hurt or sick and they didn't have any money at all. This was before any sort of programs designed to help people who really needed it. Someone at the Palava Church might suggest we all give them a pounding. That meant that everybody would bring all kinds of groceries and things to the church, and someone would take it to the people who needed it. I didn't know until recently when Frances told me that originally a pounding meant taking a pound of something like beans, cheese, butter, peanut butter or whatever.

What made the most lasting impression on me, though, were the real sick people who had no money for doctors, and who only had home remedies for cures and prayer for hope.

In these modern days, why are we not satisfied with what we have? I know a big part of the reason, but I'll save it for now.

Hard Farming

I'VE BEEN THINKING about a lot of old farming stories I've heard. Y'reckon? Yeah, I have, so here goes. After farming cotton at Palava for sixteen years, Granddaddy Rudd decided in 1916 to move his family to Champion and try ranching. I think he was always real flighty like that. (Ha ha!) He planned to sell the farm and house at Palava, but guess what? Grandmother Rudd refused to sign the papers, so they rented the farm to the people who wanted to buy it and moved on to Champion. They started ranching and all was fine until the next year when the terrible drought of 1917 set in. They came to the hard realization of how rough the cattle business can get if you don't have any farming fields to raise feed. So they loaded the wagons in January of 1918 and brought what few cattle and horses they had left to make the forty-mile trek back to Palava.

1918 was the year it didn't rain until September. That rain provided moisture enough for the cotton that had been planted in May of 1917 to come up, finally. It's hard to imagine planting cotton in May of one year and having to wait until September of the next year for it to come up! Nineteen hundred and nineteen started good and ended good. Bumper cotton crops were made, and financial times following the end of World War I were flush. Cotton was selling for a dollar a pound, and was picked off land that had cost a dollar and four bits an acre in 1900. The gin was a mile and a half away, and they thought it was practically in the field with them. Y'reckon? Yeah, they did! Why? I forgot to mention that in the early days they had taken picked cotton on a wagon pulled with a team to the Guitar Gin in Merkel. Merkel? Yeah, that's right. By going through the country it was just twenty-six miles with a team and loaded wagon. What do you think---four miles an hour?

The crop of 1919 provided money to pay off debts, mostly for land and maybe small amounts borrowed to put in a crop. I can't remember any talk of credit-card borrowing or financed amounts to go on a cruise or extended ski trip. This was some before my time, but handed-down family stories framed in my mind leave me with these ideas. Granddaddy liked good cotton and feed crops, good mules and horses, lots of family, going to church on Sunday and cold buttermilk. How was it cold, you ask? They put it in a thumb-ring gallon glass jug and let it down in the cistern water on a rope.

Nineteen hundred and nineteen created an attitude among some farmers that they would never see another poor day. They also heard the rumor that the price of cotton would go to two dollars a pound. This, of course, led to farmers pledging paid-for farms as collateral to buy more farms, and get bigger and bigger. After all, they said, cotton was going up to two dollars. This was a little less than ten years before October 29, 1929.

I said I'd say why I think we're not satisfied with what we have. Part of the reason is advertising! Publications, sign boards, radio and television have led us to believe that if we take money we don't really have and buy this (fill in the blanks), we'll be deliriously happy, popular, good-looking and rich! Y'reckon?

Lessons Hard Learned

I'VE BEEN REMEMBERING stories that Daddy told me. He was one of the better story tellers I've known. Y'reckon? Yeah, he really was. One story he told went way back, maybe to when Palava was still Center Point and didn't have a post office. It was about a man and his family who moved in from Lord only knows where. For the purpose of the story we'll say this man's name was Henry Smith. He found a place to farm but didn't have any "seed money", as they said back then. He heard about a man south of Palava who loaned money. We'll call this man Walter Jones. Mr. Smith set off that way and found Mr. Jones out in the edge of his pasture grubbing stumps so he could make his field larger. Mr. Smith told him he needed to borrow seventy dollars to put in a cotton and feed crop and also to plant a big garden. Mr. Jones said, "Go up to my house and you'll see a crock jar on the fireplace mantel. It has money in it and you can get out seventy dollars to start your farming."

Shortly after that Mr. Jones moved down south of San Angelo. Mr. Smith didn't make a crop that year, so he rode horseback to Mr. Jones's new place to tell him he hadn't made much of a crop and couldn't pay him. The next year he didn't make a good crop either, so he rode down there again and told Mr. Jones the same thing. But then, the third year when he rode to Mr. Jones's place, he told him he'd finally made a real good crop and paid him the money he owed. Let's examine this: it's about ninety miles from Palava to the south part of San Angelo. I've ridden twenty-five miles horse back in a day three or four times, and that was all I wanted. So I know that was quite a trip, times three, but the man finally paid his debt!

On October 29, 1929, the stock market crashed. That day is still known as Black Tuesday. I know of a man in Fisher County who made a pretty good cotton crop during that time. By the way, it was always interesting to me to know that back then when people had their cotton ginned they brought the bales home with them. Then when they needed money, they took a bale to town and sold it. Sometimes if a cotton buyer needed to buy a lot of cotton, he would come out and offer to buy all of someone's crop at once. Well, in the case of this man who'd made such a good crop, a buyer came out and offered him fifty cents a pound to buy the whole thing. The farmer wanted five cents more to make it fifty-five cents a pound. He decided he had enough money to make it through the next year, so he would just hold the cotton and not sell it. Then came the big market wreck, and the farmer had to sell out at the end of the next year for five cents a pound.

The daddy of a friend of mine ran a farm-lending institution back in the days we're talking about. He tells of a farmer coming in with a small amount of money to pay on his note. The man explained that their milk cow had died in spite of all they could do to save her, and the money was what the hide had brought. I had an old friend who worked here for the railroad and one who worked for a big construction company in San Antonio. Both of them have told me stories of grown family men who would go out on jobs and stay all day hoping someone would mess up and get fired and then maybe they could have that job.

During the Depression, Daddy and Mama lived at Shady Rest six miles east of Sweetwater on the east bank of Bitter Creek. They told of people who would show up in bad shape, some of them hungry. Daddy told about one man who lived in East Texas with his family. They sold all of their land, livestock and equipment and got the money in cash. They loaded up in a couple of old cars and spent four or five days moving out here to a place somewhere around Shady Rest that they knew about. All the while the man was worried about all of this cash he was carrying around, afraid he would lose it or get robbed. They finally got to their new place in the early afternoon on March 5, 1933.

The man left his family at the new place unpacking and putting up. He hurried to town to put his money in the bank before it closed for the day. The next day was March 6th, the infamous "Bankers Holiday", and the bank didn't open again. Broke? Oh no, it wasn't quite that bad---he had kept seventy cents.

How in the world can we ever possibly dare to ask why some of those old people were so hard?

. . . .

P. S. When I was in college I worked for a man named Snodgrass. He was kinda old (about my age now!) and his mother was really elderly, like early nineties. She lived in a plantation-style house. Mr. Snodgrass was a wealth of local history told to him by his grandparents who had lived through the War. He said when someone moved to Texas from Arkansas and was asked his name, when he would say, "Jones, Smith, Johnson," or whatever, the one doing the asking might say, "No, I mean what was your name before you left Arkansas?"

What Our Folks Didn't Have in 1900

LET'S JUST LOOK at what all we are blessed(?) with in 2006 that was unavailable in 1900. By the way, I am not necessarily saying that 1900 was the "good old days", as I believe we would be in a state of shock if we could go back and spend a week in March of 1900. I don't think we can imagine what the people didn't have then or what everyday life was like. Y'Reckon? Yeah, I do.

Let's approach this with something we're all familiar with--- monthly bills. We, like most of you, have just paid bills for such things as water, electricity, phones, gas, gasoline, insurance on everything but the dogs, cable TV, Internet access, web page, newspapers, magazines, book club, CD club, doctor, dentist, attorney, accountant, car and tractor repair, air-conditioner repair, electrical and plumbing repair, property taxes, state and federal taxes, and last (maybe), but certainly not least, income taxes. And let us not forget credit card payments and checks given at the mall, K-Mart, Wal-Mart, Super Giant Mart and Mart Mart, for all I know.

The fact that I was an old fogey even when I was young is a given, but hang on now. The other night Holly and I were putting property pictures on our web page (Yeah, right! Granddaddy and I killed a bear, too.) Joe called and asked Holly to bring him something to eat at work. I went with Holly to Sonic (notice I didn't say "The Sonic", like the old, uninformed folks say) and she showed me this card machine on a post under the menu where you can put in a credit card if you don't have any money. This comes under a capital red-letter heading that says, "Wrecks waiting to happen." I mean, really, now! Who wants to pay interest on a hot dog and a diet coke that they may not even remember eating?

I cooked breakfast when we got home from church Sunday. I got over into my 1900 mode and thought, "If this were 1900, they'd be cooking on a wood-burning stove. These eggs would have come from their hens, the sausage from their hogs and the milk from their cow. They would have made their own biscuits, but so did I. I guess we both bought the coffee, sugar, salt and pepper. We bought our jelly, and they made theirs."

I remember a few years back before we had a Star Discount Center, Munden's or even a Gibson's, I would notice women talking about how high their grocery bills were. Okay, they were, but now let's look in their grocery basket while we're waiting in line. Groceries and hair spray, fingernail polish, cotton balls, Pine Sol, Babo, washing powders, dish cloths, a magazine, a paper-back book and a broom. Groceries? Really, now!

Flash back to 1900 and imagine that we know what the people then would buy. Dried beans, dried fruit, flour, baking soda and baking powder, brown and white sugar, salt, pepper and vanilla. They might buy some fresh meat or pork, canned salmon, syrup, molasses, oatmeal or cream of wheat. Maybe some fresh vegetables or apples. Remember when folks used to buy pineapples and coconuts? The groceries probably cost a lot for those times, but guess what? They *were* groceries. Of all the bills we just paid, which ones did they have? Coal oil instead of electricity which includes wiring, bulbs and appliances, and on and on. What else? Maybe a doctor or dentist bill, possibly an attorney bill for a deed, will or whatever, property taxes, shoes and clothing, expenses to a lumber yard and blacksmith.

What this all adds up to is that they didn't have all of the comfort and conveniences that we have, but they also didn't have the financial responsibilities that it creates. I can't tell you what else they didn't have, but I will state the facts and you can figure it out. An income tax was levied in 1862 during the War, and lasted for about ten years. A second income tax was levied in 1894, but the Supreme Court declared it unconstitutional. In 1913 the sixteenth amendment to the Constitution allowed Congress to levy income taxes without former Constitutional restrictions. As a matter of record, one wise old politician stood up and said, "I hate to see this one per cent income tax levied because we might see the day when it would be three or four per cent." Y'Reckon?

More Things Our Grandparents Didn't Have

NOT EVERYTHING ABOUT living in our grandparents' time back in the early 1900's was good. Y'Reckon? Yeah, I do, and the more I think about it the worse it gets. So many of the deaths back then seem unusually sad to us now because we have medicines, vaccines and treatments that were unheard of then. There were so many infant deaths that we've all heard of, some in our own families. In any old cemetery you'll see a great number of graves of infants and small children. Infant mortality among Native Americans was said to be more than fifty per cent.

So many people died young back then, or so it seems now. One of my cousins died when he was twelve years old from blood poisoning, which was not all that unusual. My maternal grandmother died at forty-one from a massive heart attack. I don't think they were aware of any such problems, which was a sign of the times. My grandfather on that same side died at fifty-eight from some sort of infection, and my paternal grandfather died when he was sixty. I was told that he literally dropped dead, as my other grandmother had. Somewhere in a dark corner of my mind this brings back the title of a book called *No Time to Say Goodbye*. Papa Johnson's early death was in 1943, a long time before many studies had been made of harmful or even deadly products. It seems so ridiculous to think that a short sixty-three years ago we were comparatively in almost Dark Ages as far as environmental dangers were concerned.

To the point, at last. In 1943, the preferred method of combating boll weevils was to dust them with arsenic powder spread with a hopper similar to grass seeders attached to a tractor and driven down the rows. Say what? Envision being in short rows of cotton and continually turning back into the dust—arsenic dust, that is. No telling how many farmers died that way.

Years before this, smallpox was rampant. The Europeans brought it to the Native Americans and untold numbers of them died. In some countries more soldiers died from smallpox than died in battle. In 1796, an English physician named Edward Jenner developed a smallpox vaccine, but in spite of this wonderful discovery people were still dying of smallpox well into the twentieth century.

In 1918 and 1919, an estimated twenty million people died of influenza, 500,000 in the United States. Frances's grandfather Louis Rackley told of a family visiting them on a Sunday afternoon in 1918. While they were there the father of the family got sick and decided they'd better go home. When he left he said, "Well, Louis, I don't guess I'll see you again." He didn't. He died from the "flu", as it came to be called, and Frances's mother always remembered that his little daughter, who had been her playmate, also died.

We've had different strains of flu since then, each one a little different from the one before. In 1957 and 1958, we had the Asian flu. In 1968 and 1969 it was the Hong Kong flu. Of course these flu strains are named from the countries where they originated. We now have flu shots and antibiotics to control secondary infections that can and do add to the seriousness. By the way, the flu season in winter is actually caused by the fact that people stay inside more, with probably too many in a small place like an office, meeting room or café. Flu, like smallpox, is an airborne disease, so think about 1918 and a mother and father in a small house with several kids. It's a wonder they didn't all die. One time a friend of mine said, "I had the flu last week but I went to work anyway." I kindly said, "Let me be the first to tell you, Slim, if you were able to get up and go to work, you might have had something but you didn't have the flu."

Polio, or what was sometimes called infantile paralysis, was the dreaded disease of the 1940's and 1950's. A look back now shows that there were higher instances of it in some areas than others, and that it was sometimes crippling and sometimes not. It mostly struck children and younger folks, and it was especially terrifying because nobody knew what caused it. Finally a vaccine was developed by Jonas E. Salk, and people could rest easier. Some of our grandparents lived to see these horrible things controlled. I know Mama Johnson was born in 1882 and died in 1966, a few years after all of these things.

....

P.S. I'll try to leave on a cheerier note with a Cowpokes joke from the late 50's. A cartoon shows Slim standing by a half bed with an extra-thin mattress talking to an obviously real sick partner named Jake. He's saying, "Jake, I don't know which one's going to kill you first—the flu from Asia or the tequila from Mexico you're trying to cure it with."

TO-20

A TO-20 IS a tractor. Y'reckon? Yeah, I do. It's more commonly called a Ferguson-20, and the day Daddy bought one was a really exciting day for us. It was the first tractor I got to drive by myself. At first I was just allowed to sit on it parked and play like I was driving, and then later I could start it and back it out of the shed. After that I could drive down to check the water in the tank, and by the time I was eleven years old I could plow by myself.

Up until the time he bought the TO-20, Daddy had a Farmall F12 that he had bought new when he was farming all the time in the Thirties. He started selling Farmalls and International pickups and trucks about the time I was born. He always bought, sold and traded vehicles, tractors and equipment on his own, regardless of where he was working. He got rid of his F-12 somewhere along the way and bought and sold several 9-N Ford tractors and equipment. It seems as if the equipment was easier to change on these little tractors. The TO-20 had a two-row planter and cultivator. Then we got a blade, Fresno, one-disc terracing plow, two-disc terracing plow, five-disc Krause breaking plow, seven-disc one-way, moleboard, and a posthole digger. Daddy had kept an International five-blade tumbling stalk cutter and section harrow.

Let's examine a Ferguson TO-20. Each one came with a continental four-cylinder 20.7 horsepower motor. It had four-speed transmission and power takeoff. The front tires were 600 x 16 and the back tires were 10 x 28. These tractors weighed 2,408 pounds and the cost was

$1,568.00 plus freight. They really would plow and do a good job, but you absolutely had, I mean *had* to have the plow set right or the tractor wouldn't pull it. A lot of farmers farmed several acres with these tractors, which really didn't cost much to operate. I remember a number of good crops made with them, but the people doing it farmed all the time and never did get behind and have a big mess. The real progressive farmers had sunshades and canvas water bags on their tractors. Cleo and Eli Hennington used to build terraces to government specifications with little Ford tractors and two-disc plows. I think it took fifty-two rounds to build a terrace starting from flat ground.

After a few years with the TO-20, we got an additional tractor. It was a Jubilee Ford with five speeds and twenty-five horsepower. When we got a two-row rotary hoe for it, I could go so fast I felt like I was going to leave the ground! (Sometimes I didn't know there was any wire in the fields, but I soon found out that a rotary hoe will find it all.) Another thing I remember is pulling a two-wheel trailer behind the tractor and building fence. I've told the girls I could back a trailer before I could drive a pickup, and I could.

A lot of people want those little tractors now, and they are real neat and easy to haul. My take on that is, "We had them when they were new and it was real exciting, but that was a long time ago."

• •

P. S. One time at the Palava store they were talking about the newer Ford tractors having lights on them. Cleon Byrd spoke up and said, "After I've been on one all day, I don't need lights---I need a stretcher."

F.A.A.F.

F.A.A.F. STANDS FOR "futile attempts at farming". Y'reckon? Yeah, I do, and I should have added "I.F." for "in Fisher County"! This time of year sometimes takes me back fifty years, plus and minus a few. The other day I was looking at some Sudan (yeah, that dates me, since it's called Haygrazer now), and I was thinking that it was just "sitting there", as we sometimes say. As if we thought it might move across the road to another field! That's just one of many (I'll spare you the Latin phrase) things we say that can conjure up an unlikely image in the mind of someone who isn't from hereabouts. Anyway, the plants I'm talking about seem to be frozen in time and are no taller now than they were two weeks ago. The weeds are doing great, though. This Haygrazer, of course, was planted with a grain drill. I distinctly remember when we knew beyond a shadow of a doubt that feed had to be planted with a two-row planter set in thirty-eight-inch rows. That was just one of many "high-falutin' ideas" that didn't have a ghost of a chance. I can still hear it. "We won't be able to plow it," or "The weeds will take it plumb over." Another such wild idea was tires (or casings) without tubes in them. Absolutely ridiculous! "Why that bunch in Detroit don't know nothing." Earlier than that, we heard about trailer ball hitches. We'd hear loud testimony along the lines of, "I ain't about to pull a trailerload of yearlings to town hooked up to one of them knobs (balls). Anybody knows a trailer pin is all you can trust." This one was just good cow-sale, barbershop and café knowledge. To imagine a trailer with tubeless tires and a ball hitch was absolutely off the scale.

Uncle Herbert farmed our cotton fields and we farmed the rest of the place. "We" in reality meant me, since Daddy worked six days a week in town. I don't know how he did, but he did. Sometimes when he was on vacation he would farm some, but there were many years he wouldn't even take a vacation. A lot of those people who had been through the Depression had the mind set that if they had a job they were going to take care of it. No retirement, no insurance and no benefits, but they did have a job, and that's what counted. Anyway, about this time of year, we had very slowly and laboriously planted Sudan. The weeds were big, the Sudan was little, and the beds were big, so the furrows were deep. The beds had to be big to try to cover up the weeds that already had a good start. To try to plow it with a two-row Ford cultivator when it was that little was a joke. There won't be anybody in heaven who ever tried to plow little feed in big, tall weedy beds, especially if they tried to run fenders. Fenders were engineered to keep small plants from being covered up during cultivation. The fenders were engineered for that purpose, but designed to drive young boys nuts and cause them to have real bad, unChristian-like fits, thereby circumventing all chances of their going to the big, clean, wet feed patch up in the sky. After these attempts failed, the last-ditch effort was to pull a section harrow, which was a fun deal. You could go pretty fast, and it really would make the feed grow. But if you turned too short, the section harrow would crawl up on the back inside tractor wheel, and there you were. Seventy-five pound boys were known to hurt their backs with such doings. I may live long enough to get over it, but I haven't yet. Anyway, after a couple of times over with the section harrow, the beds would be low enough and the feed tall enough that you could plow it. That is, if you didn't put on too many sweeps. Because if you did, it converted a two-row cultivator into a real good weed rake.

Along about this time, the feed would be about waist-high and looking real good. It was easy to imagine it being head-high and real pretty. But then the cows would break into it and the old sorry fences couldn't be patched enough to hold them out, since they really didn't have much to eat in those old dried-out pastures. After all your efforts, you were about ready to haul them all to the sale, even if you had to use a trailer with a ball hitch!

Now we plant Sudan, or Haygrazer, by pulling a tandem and a grain drill. Then we watch it either grow or dry up, and we worry about it until it gets big enough to graze or bale, or until the cows break in on it. Seems a shame that we're missing so much fun!

Wash Pots

THE OTHER DAY Frances and I went to Sears to buy a new washer, dryer and refrigerator. It had been a long time since we'd had to do that, and what I saw was quite a shock to me. Y'reckon? Yeah, I do. Right off I noticed a washer and dryer that cost more than seventeen hundred dollars apiece and a refrigerator in that same price range. As I sometimes do in such cases, I went back in time. I thought, "Well, I know it was way back when I was real small and hadn't even started to school, but what I remember as a washer, dryer and refrigerator were a wash pot, a wire stretched between two posts and an icebox that the ice man delivered ice to twice a week." Man, oh man, I know that was way back when, but I remember a whole lot about it like most adults do that lived way out in the country.

When I think how it must have been, I imagine that Mama and Daddy bought that wash pot soon after they drove all the way from Palava to Hermleigh to get married in October of 1927. I wonder where they bought it and how much it cost. They probably went to Sweetwater to buy it and maybe spent a few dollars. I have no idea, but I do know the pot had a variety of uses. One time I remember Daddy going on a fishing trip and coming home with a twenty-eight pound catfish (yes, I'm sure—they weighed it on the cotton scales.) We had a big fish fry and the wash pot was used to cook the fish. I remember Mama used to make lye soap in the pot and then cut the soap up in blocks. Mainly, though, the wash pot was our only source of hot water. When Mama got ready to wash, she'd set the pot in the back yard and build a fire around it to heat water for washing clothes, and she'd rub them on a board that was standing in a wash tub. That was probably the same tub they took a bath in. After the clothes were good and clean, they were rinsed a few times and hung out on the clothesline to dry. Then they were brought in and sprinkled with water, rolled up and put in the ironing basket.

Most people had "sad irons" that they heated on a wood stove or on the burner of a coal oil-burning cook stove. (One time I asked Mama why they were called sad irons and she said she didn't know for sure but she'd always thought it was pretty difficult and sad to get the clothes ironed that way!) Washday was on Monday and then the ironing was done on Tuesday. As you can see, or in some cases remember, all of this was a long and drawn-out process. These women kept it all done, though, and still had time to do everything else. I guess the hurry, hustle and bustle we know was not common to most of those people, but I've been wondering about all they did and kept done--all the gardening, canning, sewing, cooking, cleaning and crocheting.

The icebox was a real deal and kept things cool, at least to where the milk wouldn't sour and the butter wouldn't melt. There was a tray that caught water from the melted ice, and this water was used to water flowers or whatever, but was not ever, ever to be wasted. Most people would forget from time to time to empty the water tray and it would run over. A lot of those old houses had a rotten place in the floor where the water pan had run over too many times. Now all of these things have been improved on, with washing machines that do everything except play CD's (or maybe for all I know some of them do!), electric or gas clothes dryers that do everything but fold the clothes, and super-cold part refrigerator, part freezers that dispense ice and water.

....

P. S. I wasn't looking forward to hooking up an ice maker, so I told Frances I could set a nurse bucket on top of the refrigerator with a small line running out of it to the ice maker and not have to hook up a water line as long as I remembered to keep the bucket full.

Before He Needed Lights

REMEMBER HOW I talked about how there's always some new scare? Well, sure enough, before that was even printed we had the peanut butter scare. On the television news I heard that if your peanut butter jar had a number on the back beginning with 211, the contents might be deadly. Y'reckon? Yeah, that's what they said! Now I've always considered peanut butter one of the major food groups, and being such a connoisseur I prefer Peter Pan to all other brands. I mean, to me Peter Pan is to peanut butter what Haagen-Dazs is to ice cream. I've never eaten peanut butter for breakfast, but I have eaten some a short while before dinner. (That's at noon, for those of you who don't know me.) Peanut butter is good with crackers, bread, syrup, bananas and mustard. (No, just kidding.) Mrs. Pyburn told me she had one of those 211 jars of peanut butter, but it was so nearly empty she was going to finish it. I told her I didn't know for sure but had "heard" that all the bad stuff settled to the bottom of the jar and that's what will kill you.

Now, on with the story. Fellow Lion J. D. called me early last week and said it was up to him to provide the Lions Club program. He had been all the way down his list and hadn't turned up anybody, so he called me. I later had fun giving him a hard time about being sooooo flattered to be on the bottom of the list. I told this during the program and said it reminded me of when we had a store uptown back in the middle Eighties. A girl called from the Chamber of Commerce to ask if I could go to a ribbon cutting that morning. I told her I was by myself at the moment and hadn't known I was going to be asked. She said, "They told me to call some important people first and if I couldn't get them to just call anybody." Well, at least I knew if I went I wouldn't be considered important and called on to speak or anything. NOTE: Kids will tell anything, AND some of these kids appear to be full grown.

For the Lions program I talked about old cars and some of the stories I had heard a long time ago. Daddy was a car guy from way back when. When he was real young someone took him and Mr. Bonner to Longworth from Palava so they could ride the train to Hamlin. When they got to Hamlin Mr. Bonner bought a car and Daddy taught him to drive it on the way back to Palava. It sounded like a fairly adventuresome trip. Daddy said when you bought a car back then you just got in it and drove it off---no papers, title, license or anything.

I told of hearing of two disputes about cars way back there. In one case the boys and girls in a family were planning a Saturday afternoon trip to town and were arguing about whether they'd have the windows up or down. The boys said it was so hot the windows would have to be down. The girls said the windows would have to be up to keep their hair from blowing. Finally the daddy settled it all by going out to the barn and using a cultivator foot piece to break all the windows out of the car. A similar thing happened at another house shortly after the daddy had come home with a new car on Saturday afternoon. The kids were arguing over who would get to drive it to town that night. The daddy listened awhile, then got up from the supper table and went outside. He always carried a six shooter or had one close at hand. In a minute they heard six shots, then he came back in and said he had emptied his six-shooter into the car's radiator and motor. He said he didn't figure anybody would drive it to town that night.

Another car story happened down in Atascosa County below San Antonio and was told to me by the daddy of a college roommate. He said one time a bunch of them had spent a whole day hauling whole dried peanut plants to a stationary peanut thresher, and of course they were all dirty and near total exhaustion by the end of the day. One man's car wouldn't crank in spite of all he did, and he was getting tireder and madder all the while. He went to the back of the car and got a double-bit axe out of the trunk, brought it around to the front of the car, held it up and said he was going to pull up on the crank one more time. If the car didn't start this time he was going to beat it with the axe. Well, he did, and it didn't, and he really did.

For years we heard about the unbelievable news following the day Mr. Anderson left Eskota one morning after daylight, went to the courthouse in Roby and took care of some business, then went on to Sweetwater to do some more stuff and still got back to Eskota before he had to turn his lights on. And in the whole day he only had three flats!

....

P.S. I forgot to tell y'all---what we need to be worrying about now is being wiped out by an asteroid!

Sunday Afternoon

LAST SUNDAY PUT me to thinking about what it used to be like on Sunday afternoons a long time ago. Y'reckon? Yeah, it did. The beautiful but extremely dry weather that day reminded me of the weather we had back in the Fifties. It seems like sometimes we could have some pretty, still, greening-up days following a bad sandstorm or two. After the cold weather and sand storms it was a lot more pleasant to go to church on Sunday, and Sunday afternoons were spent on activities that had probably ceased when cold weather started. The kids that had a driver's license might get to go for a ride in the country (ha ha, we WERE in the country.) The smaller kids might take a friend home with them from church or get to go home with someone else. These things usually were arranged after we got to church, since there wasn't a lot of communication in those days. This was before we had phones and most people didn't go off the farm much. Even after we had phones it seems like the lines were busy a lot of the time with six families on each party-line, and not everyone had a phone.

I can remember when it looked like Mama wasn't going to let me go home from church with someone because I had on my Sunday clothes. Usually the other boy's mother would say it was okay because her son had some extra play clothes I could borrow. It seemed like they were always way too big or little, which really didn't matter. I still think about this and sometimes when I get ready to go someplace where I need to look nice and don't think I do, I'll ask Frances if I look like I've borrowed some clothes. And then after I get home I'll say I guess I looked all right, since somebody else showed up looking like they'd borrowed clothes from not one but several different people.

Anyway, we'd get our going-home plans made and of course plan to come back to church that night, which would come all too soon. After a big Sunday dinner we'd get to go play. We might play in the barn or go down in the pasture and play. As far as I remember, all houses had a cistern, a barn, outbuildings and a storm cellar. I don't remember one that wasn't located in or on the edge of a pasture. The reason for this was that back when the house was built the people had milk cows, horses and mules that needed to be handy to the barn that was behind the house. Also, houses are easier to keep clean if they're in a pasture instead of a field.

All of this gave kids plenty of places to play if they had any imagination at all, which we mostly did. We didn't think we were entitled to be entertained. I don't think the word "bored" was even in our vocabulary. It seems like we walked around a lot. We might walk to the tank or to an old abandoned house and barn. Ditches and especially canyons were really fun. Sometime we'd walk a long way over to other people's land. We always called this "exploring". And too many times, just about the time we got our hideout or fort built so we could really play, it would be time to change clothes again and go back to church. It was fun, though.

Maybe we're still that way. The fun might be in the planning, preparing and looking forward to. Y' Reckon?

• •

P.S. I told a couple the other day that I had had an offer to buy a small part of their farm. They declined and explained that it was their home place and they lived there and still used it. I told them I really did understand. They said they might keep it a few more years and then sell it all. I said, "But that would be like selling the Alamo."

Beaver Falls, Pennsylvania

BEAVER FALLS, PENNSYLVANIA, is a long way from southeast Fisher County. Y'reckon? Yeah, I do. It's 1275 miles as the crow flies, or even as the chicken walks. I mention this because there was a plaque (I did say *was*, as in past tense) mounted on the truss work of the Sweetwater Creek Bridge northeast of the Eskota Road that read "Penn Bridge Company Builders 1891".

Now, let's go back in our mental time machine and picture this bridge being built. First off, I imagine the bridge builders were already in this part of Texas building no telling how many bridges. They would have arrived by train with their crew of engineers, foremen, carpenters, blacksmiths, rivet setters and cement workers. No cranes, backhoes, Lincoln welders, ready-mix trucks or nail guns. They probably designed the bridge first and then mailed orders home for the sizes and amount of steel they would need. This material would be delivered eventually by T&P Railway to the Eskota train station. (All trains going west stopped at Eskota to "coal up" so as to make it up the grade to Sweetwater.) Maybe the lumber and cement for the project were also shipped with the steel. All this had to be moved from Eskota to Sweetwater Creek by freight wagon. Sweetwater Creek, by the way, is a real creek. It heads up north of Maryneal in central Nolan County, cuts across southeast Fisher County, and goes into the Clearfork of the Brazos River a little way over in Jones County northwest of Noodle.

The bridge builders might have stayed in the hotel at Eskota or in a boarding house, but they very likely camped on Sweetwater Creek and had their own cook, like in a mining or cow camp. They had to have all their own tools to dig, saw, hammer and mix cement, as well as a block and tackle and very likely their own teams to raise the steel with pulleys and ropes. After all, you couldn't hire just anyone with an unknown team to raise steel above men's heads. They had to have their own portable blacksmith shop and forge. All the steel in the bridge was put together with rivets, lots and lots of rivets, or, to say it more properly, buckets and buckets of rivets. You see, the blacksmith kept the rivets hot in a forge, then his helper used tongs to put a few in a bucket so he could carry them to the man with the rivet-setting tool (like a concave punch) and hammer. The helper put the rivet in the hole with tongs while it was red hot so the rivet setter could set it. (You'd want to go to the gym early and stay late if you were studying on "arm rasslin'" the rivet setter!)

The lumber was 3" x 12" rough-sawed bridge timbers that could be set close together crosswise and then some longwise for wagon wheels to roll over. From its completion in 1891 until the first automobile crossed it might have been fifteen or twenty years. My builder's mind will not allow me to think of these men as building a bridge---it was more on the order of creating a creek crossing. Back then towns and communities were separated by creeks and rivers, sometimes for a long time. Folks walked, waded or swam across them on foot or horseback, drove or floated wagons across, or just stayed on the other side.

Beaver Falls, Pennsylvania, continued

ONE TIME ODIE Stribling, foreman on the Catfish Ranch founded by the Newman brothers ten years or so before the Eskota bridge was built, told some of us young aspiring cowboys a good story. After we had penned a bunch of uncooperative black Brangus cattle who had a strong objection to being penned, we got to hear the story. Y'reckon? Yeah, we did.

Odie said the Newmans had bought a big bunch of two-year-old horned steers out of Louisiana and had them shipped on cattle cars to the Eskota railroad pens. He and an assortment of horseback cowboys rode from one of their pastures about three miles north of Eskota to meet the train and bring the steers home. Years later Odie still remembered sitting on a horse in the middle of Wallace Street, now called CR170, where it crossed Elm Street, now CR168, which runs north, waiting for the steers to be let out. When the gate opened, he took off. He loped his horse up Elm Street, going in front of the store on the left and the bank on the corner of Elm and Hogg Streets, on across Trent Street, by the school on the right, across Lindsey Street and on across the bridge, and eventually into the pasture, with the steers following him all the way. He said that was the easy part. The hard part came a year or two later when they had to round those steers up and go back to the railroad pens. The market then was for four-or-five-year-old grass-fat steers.

Sometimes I think about the bridge and all the people who have crossed it---on foot, on horseback, in wagons, on tractors and in vehicles, and the people who have fished off of it or camped, picnicked or played under it. I remember when it still had bridge timbers for a floor put together with 60 penny nails. That pennyweight means each nail weighs three ounces (once a teacher. . .), and you don't drive those with the dollar-ninety-nine-cent hammer you got out of the bargain bin at the discount store.

I guess by now you're somewhat prepared for the short sad story that not long ago someone who was probably on the wrong road, driving an oilfield work-over unit that was too tall and powerful, took down so much of the bridge's overhead truss that the remainder had to be cut down for scrap iron. Steve Mahaffey has a crew rebuilding the bridge but not the overhead truss. The floor has been concrete for the last several years and the truss isn't really necessary. When the floor was wooden it made all sorts of horror-house noises, different noises according to whether it was wet or dry. They are going to put the original plaque back, though. That's good.

Over the years people have stopped at one end of the bridge or the other to let someone else come across first. It's not unusual for them to say, "Howdy," and even stop to talk and exchange news of families, cattle, farming or neighbors. Imagine, in the early times this might have happened once a week, later on maybe once a day, and now it's back to maybe once a week. If our time machine told us the stops had averaged three times a week, that totals nearly 18,000 times.

The other day I stopped on the west end of the bridge. Richard Broadwell was emptying a rain gauge. We each gave our rain reports and then we cleaned out tanks, built fence, bought and sold cattle, located rubber boots and planted native grass. Before, during and after this we talked about the bridge. We heartily agreed that the bridge to some people might be just Fisher County Bridge #168-1, but to us and a bunch more country folks it's a hundred and fifteen years of history.

....

P.S. Water is always such an issue in our country. I don't believe I have ever seen anyone cross the Eskota bridge without looking down at the creek. That tells a lot.

Sunday Socks

A LONG TIME ago, back during my growing up days, people had Sunday socks. Y'reckon? Yeah, they did. As a matter of certain fact, they had a lot of Sunday things. There were Sunday shoes, Sunday pants, Sunday shirts, Sunday jackets, and on and on and on. The things I'm talking about were, of course, the dress-up clothes that most people only wore on Sunday. When they got home from church, they took those nice clothes off to be put away for the next Sunday. Then the kids had school clothes and of course everyone had everyday clothes and work clothes. I used to work with an old fellow who still referred to the things he put on to go to town on Saturday afternoon as "going-somewhere clothes".

Sundays were really Sundays back then, as in special days. Practically every one we knew of put on Sunday clothes and went to Sunday school and church. Some of the women cooked early and left the food in the oven, or even left it cooking in the oven, which could cause a great deal of consternation if the preacher preached too long or if anything held up the church service. Big Sunday dinners were the order of the day. Going out to eat was practically unheard of. It seems like pot roast, mashed potatoes and gravy was kind of a winter-time thing and fried chicken and vegetables from the garden was more of a summer-time meal. After Sunday dinner, the smaller children played out in the yard or around the barn. In the summer they might get to go swimming in the tank. The older kids might, and I did say *might*, occasionally get to go to town and ride around burning up twenty-cent gasoline. The grown men usually sat out on the porch and read a newspaper if they had one. Once in awhile they might drive around close by and look at crops. Sometimes if the weather was good they might go visit kinfolks. Seems as if everyone had a lot of kinfolks. Of course, as I've said before, listening to the radio was a big thing, but I remember that as being more of a winter pastime when the weather was cold. On in the summer, Sunday afternoons might be prime watermelon-eating time.

Some of the older ones of the cowboy set might have a roping arena where they gathered on Sunday afternoon. The next time I'm plowing at the farm, I'm going to try to remember how many roping arenas were around out there. I even remember one arena out on the east end of what is now Seventeenth Street, or County Road 119, but I can't remember whose it was. The plan was always to get a bunch of crossties and some net wire and build a big arena. There would have to be some lumber for the roping chute and box. Some of the fancier arenas had a calf return alley and maybe even an elevated announcer's stand. They might have four tall posts and a bucking barrel somewhere outside the arena. Some boy would clear off a place and get all of his friends to help him build an arena. This was a tremendous amount of work. They would all rope together for a while and then get crossways. One of them would build another arena somewhere else and a few would split off and go over to the new one. It always reminded me of groups in churches splitting off and starting a new church and then maybe a bunch of them splitting again. I don't recollect many split-offs of any kind working for very long.

Late on Sunday afternoon it was time to get ready to go back to church. I guess this reaches back a lot farther than I do, but I really do remember at certain times of the year, when the Sunday morning service was ending, hearing the preacher say, "Thank all y'all for coming and we'll see you back here about twilight time."

• •

P.S. I would be proud to claim this if it were mine, but it's not. So, to kinda, sorta quote one of my favorite writers: "Grandmother always said, 'Sundays were when the women stayed in the kitchen to fry chicken and talk about the Lord. The men sat out on the porch and talked about politics and farming. It always seemed like the women and the Lord got more done.' "

Weather

Storms

WE'VE JUST ABOUT seen it all on television now. Y'Reckon? Yeah, I do. First, a few years ago we watched a war while it was happening, and now we've seen a hurricane in progress and then another one not much later. I guess everybody in the country was keeping up with the progress of that last storm on television. The tracking of it was minute by minute. I thought about that, and then I realized how much things have changed in the last hundred plus years. As you know, the record-breaking hurricane was in 1900. It hit Galveston and killed an estimated six thousand people. I couldn't help thinking, I don't guess they had any idea in the world that such devastation was coming their way. Can't you imagine that when the wind force got up to fifty miles an hour they thought that was the height of it? But then it went on to sixty miles an hour and seventy-five miles an hour, and on and on until I guess it passed the point of making any difference because everything was destroyed. But it boggles the mind to think that they had no earthly idea of the force that was on its way. Can't you imagine the mindset of the survivors in that area? Every time the wind got up pretty high after that, they could think another horrible hurricane was on its way. Of course, the two hurricanes that have just happened, Katrina and Rita, took way too many lives and caused so much wreckage. And on a lesser scale, think of all the ruined vehicles, tractors, boats, travel trailers, pets, horses, cattle and crops.

We hear about and see the destruction of the big towns, but there are so many smaller towns and communities that are seriously damaged or simply gone completely. Our youngest daughter Alison lives in Stillwater, Oklahoma, with her husband Jamey. His family members mostly live in Kountze, twenty miles north of Beaumont. Last week when he knew Rita was coming, Jamey wanted them to come to Oklahoma to be safe, but they weren't sure they wanted to do that. Finally, after a couple of days of trying to decide what to do, Jamey's parents Jody and Sandy made up their minds to go. Nana and Papaw, Sandy's parents, just didn't want to leave their home—their choice was to stay there and brave the storm. And his brother Danny, a Beaumont policeman, didn't have a choice—he and all the rest of the force were placed on indefinite duty. The trip to Oklahoma took Jody and Sandy twenty hours, even though they'd made sure to have a full gas tank and some extra cans of gas in the pickup bed. That's just how slowly the traffic was moving.

Frances and I had followed the whole thing from here, and were so relieved when Alison called us Saturday morning during the Abilene Book and Author Festival to let us know everybody down in Kountze and Beaumont had made it through the storm all right. The shingles were all blown off Sandy and Jody's home and all their big trees had blown down, but at least none of them fell on the house. I knew Jody had built that house to stay. I just worried about flooding and about trees falling. Their oldest son Danny lives in the original house nearby on the same acreage, and his house is still standing, too, even though his roof is damaged. He can't get off to check on it or make repairs, though—the Beaumont police are patrolling in truck beds and living off peanut butter and crackers, honey buns and warm water. All the shingles were blown off Nana and Papaw's house, and the roofs are gone off all their outbuildings, but they're all right.

It's really hot here and the forecast says it will be hot all week, which will only make it drier, but you know what…? That may not be as bad as we thought!

Dry

I THINK MOST everybody realizes by now that it's dry. Y'reckon? Well, I'm not sure. As usual, there's probably somebody who hasn't noticed yet! Back in early December, I was saying that I really didn't know what to think about this dry spell, because it just *felt* different to me. As if that had any credence. Since then I've been reading some weather history in a book by Charlie Jordan, where he tells some facts about dry. Here's one: Bagdad, California, suffered a dry spell to beat them all. Not a drop of rain fell there from October 3, 1912, to November 8, 1914. That's 767 days. Two years, one month and five days. Y'reckon anybody was left there to see it?

A few years back, a friend of mine and I were in Terlingua where it had rained just nine-tenths of an inch in the preceding twelve months. And in 1956, the town of Wink, Texas, had only 1.76 inches of rain for the whole year. Since we had a sandstorm on New Year's Day this year, the following story caught my eye. In 1965, a dust storm that originated near Lubbock sent dust up to 31,000 feet and reduced visibilities to 100 yards in places west of a line from Tulia to Abilene. When the storm was over, it was discovered that the rain gauge at Reese Air Force Base contained not rain but three inches of fine sand!

Enough of the dry. Before we get too down about it, let's talk about some really good rains. In the first four days of August, 1978, Albany received the record-breaking Texas rain of 29.05 inches. Abilene only received six inches that time. And I think I heard that Eskota got three-tenths and Newman got a trace. (I'm making this Eskota and Newman part up. But, I really wouldn't doubt it at all. It's always so dry there.)

Back in 1932, Mama and Daddy lived at Shady Rest, about four miles down Bitter Creek from the Sweetwater Lake Dam. The dam was new and not quite finished when it rained eleven inches in one night. Mama and Daddy were worried all night that the dam might not hold. The rain filled Sweetwater Lake that night and the dam did hold. There was a scraper left in the lake that, of course, was covered with water. A scraper is an old-timey piece of equipment that is on wheels and has a blade like a maintainer and has to be pulled with a dozer. By the time I was old enough to hear this story twenty years later, I was led to believe there was more equipment in the bottom of the lake than we have working on Broadway now. Such is the way of most stories that do have a small base of truth. And as I've said before, on the night of May 23, 1957, we had over eleven inches of rain to end the drought that had started in 1950.

I don't know anyone who sees a big rain coming now, but, after all, they obviously didn't see one coming in 1932, either. And I don't know but what everybody had about lost all hope before it finally rained in 1957. We're overdue for one of these big record-breaking rains. Just the other day a man told me he didn't even care if it came a big hail storm just so long as it was real wet hail!

Have We Possibly Outsmarted Ourselves?

SOMETIMES I HAVE a fleeting glimpse that we may have outsmarted ourselves with all our new-found, ever-advancing high technology that gets higher and higher. Y'reckon? Yeah, I do. A man told me the other day, "I don't know what I'm gonna do. My kids are not young enough now to work this stuff that's coming out." That sounds funny at first, but then you think, "Now, wait a minute! If the young adults can't work it, reckon where that puts my peer group?" I think the formula for us reads: young adults times two plus x.

We have an ever-growing number of hyper, high-strung, jerky, ticky, or, as the old folks used to say, fractious folks. The number is actually growing. We have more counselors, therapists, places for folks to go and get all the knots out of their rope, tranquilizers, go-fast pills, uppers, downers, and maybe even sideways-ers for folks that would be happy just to tread water.

Hang on, now---this is fixing to go a little bit farther than planting straight rows of black-eyed peas. It is believed that some prehistoric people like Alley-Oop and his friends started using fire about 500,000 B. C. About 100,000 B. C. they started making special tools for cutting, chopping and scraping. They began to sew primitive clothes about 15,000 B. C. The first farmers lived in Israel and Jordan about 9,000 years ago. (And here I grew up thinking the first farmers were in Fisher County!) They lived in family groups of about twenty-five to fifty people and probably never saw another group. It's estimated that only a few thousand people lived in Africa and a similar number in Asia. By about 3,500 B. C. people became better farmers and could grow enough food to support small villages. Shortly before 3,000 B. C., writing was invented in the Tigris-Euphrates valley in what is now Iraq. This began the recording of history, and prehistoric times came to an end.

Okay, so that means it took us about half a million years to evolve from fire to tools to clothes to farming to villages to writing. Now, we've known people who came here on a wagon, covered or not, and lived to see a man on the moon. This evolved in just one lifetime. And now my generation has lived from maybe not even having a phone to carrying one all the time, from typewriters and carbon paper to word processors, from post cards to electronic mail. From cooking on a wood or kerosene stove to microwaves, from peaches off the tree to instant pudding. From hard-ground front yards to instant grass, from basic cars to cars that talk to you. From hand-written ledgers to computer printouts. From Kodak box cameras with six exposures to digital cameras that show you the picture right now and are like Hollywood six-shooters---you don't have to reload them.

I think sometimes that the computer-technology-gadget age has run way far out of bounds for the normal process of evolution. It strikes me as being like if all of a sudden we only worked ten hours a week, took a pill instead of eating, slept ten hours a week and had cars that would run three hundred miles an hour and were kept in a climate-controlled garage. I really think this is kinda sorta what has happened to us, and our minds and our emotions, or our very "being", if you will, have not caught up with it and are rebelling. You think? Put that in your pipe and smoke it awhile.

Precious

I REMEMBER A few years back when playing word association games was pretty much the "in" thing to do. Y'reckon? Yeah, I do. It went something like this: "When I say a word you say the first thing that comes into your head." So then I'd say "red" and you might say "fire truck", or "watermelon". Let's say we're going to play that game now and I'll start by saying "precious". You might say "kitten". (Okay, Granny, I know, you would say "my grandbaby".) Or some country boy like me might say "coon dog puppy", when what we all should be saying right now is "water." Yeah, really. We can't get around that one.

When I was in college back in the early Sixties I read an article in a real good magazine (probably cost fifty cents) that said by the end of the century we'd be in a concerning water shortage in the Southwest. There was even a picture of a dry tank. We have plenty of those now. The picture showed a canteen pointing open end down on the side of the dam with the lid off and no water coming out of it. It seems absolutely amazing that the people responsible for that article knew then where we were headed. Why didn't we take heed?

Let's weigh this a little and think about what we as living things cannot, I mean absolutely cannot live without. Of course, what we're talking about is water. I mean, there are things we'd like to have, things we want to have, things we may even need to have. But we have to have water or we cannot survive. I was talking with some friends the other day and they mentioned a town in New Mexico that has only a 120-day water supply left. Then we wondered, "What would those people think about us watering our yards, washing our pickups and cars, or, in my case, washing my stock trailer?" We just know they would see us as being extremely wasteful, and you know what? It looks like we are. One morning last week I was walking before daylight and saw "precious" running down the gutter on 17th Street. It's all something to think about. We're truly blessed with our water wells and have better water than before. But the water wells, just like the lakes, have to be replenished by rainfall, as in abundant rainfall.

Let me leave you with this thought. Gasoline is presently $2.84 per gallon. Water by the per-each bottles that are so popular figures about $7.50 per gallon. We don't have to have gasoline. No, really, we don't. The world will turn, the sun will rise and set, and we'll still be here to see it if we don't have gasoline. But water . . .?

The Dust Bowl

I'VE BEEN READING a bunch of stuff on Great Plains history dealing with droughts, the Stock Market Crash of 1929, the Dust Bowl, and United States government agriculture reports from that time. The area covered by the Dust Bowl was immense---it took in parts of Nebraska, Kansas, Colorado, New Mexico and parts of the Texas Panhandle, and the storms crossed four major rivers: Arkansas, Cimarron, Canadian and Red. Reading about all that was such a downer that I had to watch the Three Stooges to balance things out. Y'reckon? Yeah, I do. I remember hearing Mother and Daddy talking some about the Dust Bowl, but not much. They talked about chickens going to roost in the middle of the day because the sandstorms would make it so dark, but that was about the extent of it. And that was told in the early to mid-Fifties when we were again in a drought and had a lot of sandstorms.

One of the first recorded accounts of anyone crossing the Great Plains was in 1541 by Francisco Vasquez de Coronado, who was looking for the Seven Cities of Gold. He spent the winter of 1540 in Tiguex, a Pueblo village on the Rio Grande below the village of Taos. In the spring he divided his three hundred or so men into three groups. They really swung a wide loop, being the first Europeans to travel on the Rio Grande and find the Grand Canyon. They also traveled in the Texas Panhandle and were the first Europeans to discover the Palo Duro Canyon near present-day Amarillo and on up past where Dodge

City is now. (Boy, they better be glad Festus didn't get wind of it!) Oh, no, once again I've wandered off the subject.

People came to the Great Plains for varied reasons, just like they did anywhere else. It was a haven for respiratory ailments. For awhile one area was so full of English-accented citizens moving away from the industrial smog in England that it was called Little London. The Great Plains covered millions upon millions of acres of native grass that held the rich soil together even in extremely dry years. It was home to buffalo, antelope, deer, grouse, prairie chickens and more. It was also the home of the Comanche, Kiowa, Apache and many other Indian tribes. The grass thrived, allowing the buffalo and other game to thrive as well and in turn for all the Native Americans to thrive.

All was well for centuries, scores, decades and more until about the time the War was over in 1865, and then things started to unravel. All manner of small and large changes came with the pioneers, the settlers, the ranchers, the soldiers, the scalp hunters and, most devastating, the buffalo hunters. The buffalo hunters struck the hardest blow to all the tribes of "the staked plains" in 1872 and 1873 when a reported twenty-five million buffalo were killed. This whole scenario, from the pioneers of the eighteen hundreds who plowed up millions of acres of native grass, to the worst recorded sandstorm of all time on what is known as Black Sunday, April 14, 1935, is the best example I've ever known of or studied about to support the saying, "If it ain't broke, don't fix it."

Following the devastation of the land, things changed with the scattering of Indians living there. It was the Red River War of 1874-75 that broke the Comanche, who, when horseback were known as the best light-horse cavalry in the world. In one battle in Palo Duro Canyon six army columns attacked a Comanche encampment, catching them by surprise. The Comanche who lived fled, and the army slaughtered 1048 horses, leaving the "Lords of the Plains" afoot and hungry. In this condition they were no match for General Philip T. Sheridan and his troops.

Quanah Parker, son of white captive Cynthia Ann Parker and Chief Peta Nocona, was chief of the Comanche at the time. He stayed on, living on a reservation in Indian Territory, Oklahoma. He founded a native religion based on vision quest through the hallucinogens peyote and mescal, a religion which the Supreme Court upheld as a protected form of worship. In later years Quanah had a large house of seven apartments because he had seven wives. The government Indian agent assigned to him as advisor and friend had to have a talk with him one day. I imagine it went something like this: "Quanah, you have made great strides to become civilized. You don't raid and steal horses any more, and you live in a house and grow a garden. But civilized people such as we just have one wife, so you need to pick out your favorite wife and tell the others to go on and leave." It was reported as fact that Quanah looked straight at the agent an uncomfortably long time and finally said, "You tell'em."

The XIT

IN 1870 THE powers in control of Texas decided they needed a grandiose state house in Austin. Y'reckon? Yeah, they did. They got to thinking about how it was now fifteen years after the War, and things were getting better all the time. Then, in typical Texas fashion, they further decided that their state house should be the biggest one in the union and should be built out of polished red granite. In order to pay for this big splash, the state offered to give three million acres in the Texas Panhandle to anybody who would build the capitol building. The Panhandle was a desirable and flourishing location at the time because Charles Goodnight had moved fifteen hundred cattle from Colorado to Palo Duro Canyon, and the free grass there had attracted other cattlemen and speculators from two continents.

In 1882 the Capitol Syndicate from Chicago took title to the three million acres, and this became the famous XIT Ranch. The capitol building they planned to build in Austin would cost 3.7 million dollars, which meant the XIT land must be worth a dollar and twenty-three cents an acre. The syndicate's purchase attracted attention from members of the British Parliament and others, including the Earl of Aberdeen, who thought it was worth their long-distance investment. In England, books immediately came out about how you could double your money on the High Plains of Texas. It's hard for us now to fathom that there wasn't anything there, just three million acres of grass. The sight of it was often compared to looking out over the ocean. The Panhandle area itself covered about twenty million acres, with more than 460 species of native Texas grasses.

By 1887 the XIT had nearly eight hundred miles of fence, over three hundred windmills, and 150,000 head of cattle. When the railroad shipping points came to the ranch, they soon became towns. These towns brought merchants and all sorts of other people. Working on the XIT was a good life for a thirty-dollar-a-month cowboy. Gambling, drinking, and shooting anything without permission were prohibited on the ranch itself, but around its borders little rail towns with little or no law sprang up. The town of Dalhart was started in 1901 at the intersection of two railroads, one north to Denver and the other east to Liberal, Kansas.

Even with dollar and twenty-three cent-per-acre land and thirty-dollar-a-month cowboys, the XIT had trouble making a profit. The ranch suffered floods, hailstorms, blizzards, drought, grass fires, and tornadoes. The winter of 1885-86 nearly wiped out cattle herds on the southern Plains, and the next winter did the same thing up north from there. The British investors wanted a better return on their money, so they turned to the help of local promoters who started offering farms for thirteen dollars an acre. They gave free rides to the area from Kansas City to prospective buyers, as many as five hundred at a time. This was a bi-monthly event. Advertising read, "Get a farm in Texas while land is cheap---where every man is a landlord!" They published books of advice that promised, if followed, to guarantee prosperity. They said that plowing of the land itself would bring rain, and rain follows the plow! Dust mulch was supposed to hold moisture in the ground. The cold fact, regardless of all this propaganda, was that the average annual rainfall there was sixteen inches. This land would need twenty to twenty-two inches per year at the right time to be productive. There would actually be a few scattered years where this could happen, but there were also some ten and twelve-inch years.

Up above the XIT and in "No Man's Land" in Oklahoma, the government offered extended homesteads (320 acres instead of 160 acres) and by 1914 fifty-three thousand claims had been made over the Great Plains. By 1926 all but 450,000 acres of the XIT had been sold and plowed up, as well as millions upon millions of acres of Plains grassland above it.

High Plains Wheat---Boom to Bust

THE XIT RANCH covered three million acres in 1882. Y'reckon? Yeah, I do. It was part of a huge area of native grass that had been there for thirty-five thousand years. This grassland covered twenty-one per cent of the United States and Canada. It was part of the great plow-up that started at the turn of the century and continued until 1930. One man near Dalhart had thirty-five thousand acres of plowed-up prairie sod to plant wheat on. By 1912, all but 450,000 acres of the old XIT had been plowed up. The Texas Panhandle had about 800,000 acres that had been plowed up by 1924, but this increased to 2.5 million acres by 1929. So the plowing up was all over the Great Plains. When all this plowing up of native grass was complete, the area plowed covered parts of five states and over 100 million acres.

The farmers and speculators, lots of them, came from everywhere to get in on the money-making. About 12,000 Russian Germans came to Kansas. Most of them brought a little wheat seed with them, sometimes sewn into the linings of their coats. This was a hard red wheat seed like they were used to growing, and it was hardy and productive. What they didn't realize was that mixed in with some of this wheat seed was another tiny seed that came from the Russian thistle, or tumbleweed. These are green weeds in growing season, but after a frost dries them up they can blow for miles, and every time they bounce on the ground they lose seed that will grow another bunch of thistles.

This plowed-up prairie was rich and productive. One woman with 2,000 acres of wheat reported an income of $75,000 one year. In those early times, wheat cost thirty-five cents a bushel to produce, and was selling for $2.25 a bushel. With such stories as that going around, the race was on to plow up more grass and plant more wheat. One man in eastern Colorado decided to get rich plowing up grassland. He bought a new 1929 model tractor and the biggest plow available that would disc a ten-foot swath at a time. Everything looked good, and of course they had no reason to think it wouldn't go on forever. But just about the time they finished planting in the fall of 1929, there came the well-known Stock Market Crash on October 29.

It turned out the farmers had planted wheat to their own detriment. There was no place for so much. Wheat prices started to go down from $2.25 a bushel, so the wheat farmers, unable to believe it wouldn't come back, just planted twice as much ground trying to make up. It didn't, though, and in the Thirties one man reported that he had gone to the wheat elevator and found wheat bringing eighty cents a bushel, but by the time he cut his wheat and got back to the elevator with it, the price had dropped to twenty-four cents.

Things got even worse, in that it got to the point where you couldn't sell wheat at all. People were burning it in their stoves, instead of wood or coal. And wheat prices weren't the only ones to drop. Oil went from $1.43 a barrel to ten cents. A dozen eggs could bring as little as six cents. One man traded sixteen dozen eggs for a new pair of overalls. Eight million people were out of work, to make an unemployment rate of twenty-nine per cent. Eleven thousand people lost all their savings, and nine thousand banks completely failed. One of these was the United States Bank of New York, with two hundred million in deposits.

It Turned Dry and the Wind Started to Blow

IN 1931, WHEAT farmers nationwide produced their biggest crop ever. Y'reckon? Yeah, I do. It was 250 million bushels! Up in the Texas Panhandle they were piling wheat on the ground near the full elevators next to the piles from the year before. After awhile, armed farmers were turning back other farmers trying to haul in wheat. They were trying to get their own wheat sold, but the effort was futile. There were no buyers for the wheat. There was no money to buy it, nor anywhere to send it. And prices had declined drastically due to the impact of a world depression. The wheat was in rotting piles all over the Great Plains. This situation was partly due to the U. S. Food Administrator's having established a price guarantee of two dollars a bushel back during the Great War, the same guarantee that had caused more and more grassland to be plowed up for wheat production. Now the farmers tried desperately to get price support from Washington. When this failed, they started "The National Farmers' Holiday," asking people to stay home and not buy or sell anything. That was a pitifully hollow threat, since nobody was able to do either of those things anyway.

The year 1932 was too dry to plant in most areas, so there was little or no ground cover. And then the wind began to blow. When it got to blowing twenty-five or thirty miles an hour, dry dirt started to move, and as the wind speed increased dust storms were born.

Tumbleweeds broke loose and piled against fences, which started the sand to piling up. The dust got into homes, barns, cars, everything. It was in the water, the food, the furniture, cabinets and beds. People put wet sheets over windows and doors trying to keep it out. They swept their houses out daily, and still more dust came. They put up picket fences and covered them with canvas to protect gardens that were watered from windmills. After years of this, the cattle and horses were gone, the pigs and chickens, too, because they didn't have anything to eat. Static electricity could be seen playing on windmill towers and would even cause car engines to stall. It killed the gardens and turned them black. Schools were often closed and many stores abandoned because it was so hard to get to them. Cars ran into each other on the roads because the drivers couldn't see, or because one car was stuck in a sand drift on the road. The hospitals and Red Cross stations were full of people with dust pneumonia, which was ironic since some people with lung problems had come there in the first place looking for a better, drier climate.

The first of the big dust storms was recorded on January 21, 1932, when a cloud ten thousand feet high appeared north of Amarillo, moving up the Texas Panhandle and on into Oklahoma, Colorado and Kansas. The wind speed reached sixty miles an hour. These storms came to be called Black Blizzards. The Oklahoma Panhandle had six of them in the winter of 1932. Summer came hot and dry that year, with one place in Colorado registering 115 degrees. It rained twelve inches that year.

The Texas Panhandle had more than seventy severe dust storms in 1933. On May 11, 1934, one of these storms reached all the way to New York City, where the Statue of Liberty was barely visible for five hours. The dust from these storms went two hundred miles out to sea after leaving dust in the White House and in Chicago, Boston and Philadelphia. 1934 was the worst year for the dust storms. Parts of Nebraska that had been lucky so far got dry and real hot. Fields that had produced twenty bushels were down to one bushel per acre. One county in upper Colorado that had produced five million bushels now produced five thousand. Eight million acres did not produce at all, and two million were fallow. These states had high winds and little rain, so things were much the same as with earlier dust storms in the lower states.

April 14, 1935, came to be known as "Black Sunday." This was the day of the worst of all the sandstorms. A pilot who had taken off from the Texas Panhandle saw the storm coming and climbed to 23,000 feet trying to get above it before giving up and going back to the airport to land. (Side note—that pilot was Amelia Earhart.) By Monday, the remains of Black Sunday were blowing east and south into the Gulf of Mexico. It's hard to imagine topsoil blowing at sixty-five miles an hour from an area approximately five hundred miles long north and south and three hundred miles wide east and west. This storm was the last straw for a lot of people. More and more families left their farms, businesses and towns. Some towns discontinued city services completely. More than sixty per cent of farms and businesses had unpaid taxes. Dalhart recorded over a hundred and thirty sandstorms that year. There was just nowhere to get that was free of dust, nowhere to go to take a deep breath.

As one old dyed-in-the-wool distraught Texas Panhandle cowboy said looking down at the ground, "No wonder it's blowing. It's wrong side up."

Weather

EVERYONE TALKS ABOUT the weather but no one does anything about it. Y'reckon? Yeah, I do. And that's also one of Samuel Clemens's famous sayings. (Yeah, you do—that's Mark Twain!) Of course the weather is just one of many things that people talk but do nothing about.

The turn of the year is usually a big important time to weather buffs. It takes a good hand hereabouts to get even close to being correct with weather predictions. I myself have always had great aspirations in this direction but probably won't ever get there. However, I do have a couple of men I talk to that are pretty good. They have more experience than I do and are more observant, too. And besides all that, they're originally from Fisher County! When it's been as dry as it has been off and on, mostly for the last several years, correctly predicting weather becomes increasingly difficult no matter how much you know. Sometimes it gets down to very unscientific things such as "just a feeling" about it. I know it's almost laughable, but back at the start of our present extended dry spell I told Frances, "This one just feels different." I may have to rely on things like that, since I have little knowledge and no training or formal education in such matters.

The other day a friend of mine reminded me about what I call the English way of predicting weather for the coming year, a system that started in England centuries ago. Each of the first twelve days of the year represents a corresponding month, so that the weather on January first is supposed to be a forecast for January, on January second for February, and so on. In his book *Puro Mexicano* J. Frank Dobie wrote of a similar system that originated in Old Mexico using the whole first thirty days of the year. It's on a chart in three columns and is really pretty good. I kept these charts for twenty years or so but the weather has been such a wreck lately that I've quit for now.

Then there's the Easter one that's supposed to be Native American and is really pretty good, too. So far I've just seen it work on the bad or real bad side. This one is all read on the direction that smoke is blowing from a smoldering fire during the time the first ray of sun appears until the sun is fully up on the eastern horizon. The "worst" it can be is for the smoke to be blowing straight east because that means the wind is straight out of the west. I've already seen enough results of that and it was bad, real bad.

The Texas Southwest Cattle Raisers Association monthly report in November stated: Forty per cent of Australia's crop-growing region is experiencing the worst drought in the last one thousand years. How do they know? They didn't say--I just always thought folks in Australia knew a lot. After all, it's even drier there than it is in Eskota and Newman.

On our local brighter side, I can tell you that on New Year's Day the wind was out of the east and that just has to be good. One of the men of whom I am a protégé told me that we've had some wet years that ended in seven. The highly-paid weather forecasters and the writers of the almanac are saying we're headed into wetter times. Maybe I'd better air up the trailer tires to haul some cattle from the sale instead of to the sale. Oh! I nearly forgot. You asked who are the guys I depend on when the roads get rough and the fields dry? It's Mr. Ballard and Mr. Pyburn. But don't tell them I told you!

More Weather

IT'S NOT UNCOMMON for us to have bad weather right at the turn of the year. Y'reckon? Yeah, I do. I can remember several such spells. In the winter of 1949 we had a real bad ice storm and a lot of big mesquite trees broke down. School was out for a few days because the buses couldn't run. Carroll Kearney from Palava said his family was out of electricity for three weeks or more. They had recently bought a deep freeze and filled it with food, but the food in it never did spoil during that time. They just kept it closed in the daytime and open at night.

I think it was in 1972 when we had another such spell and people were stranded here in Sweetwater. There were about three hundred trucks shut down out at the Union 76 truck stop. Most of the trucks were left running, but the ones that were turned off were really hard to start again. All the motels were full, even the Ranch House where there wasn't any heat. I was welding at the time and we were out there completely rebuilding the boiler that supplied their heat. We had to replace all fifty-two of the boiler flues, which meant that by the time we finished the ice spell was over.

We had another bad spell right along at Christmas in 1984. People had trouble Christmas shopping because they couldn't get around. I had a four-wheel-drive pickup named Billy Burl, so Frances and I went to Anthony's and TG&Y to do our Christmas shopping. That wasn't really what we had planned, but it was the best we could do. If they didn't have it there, we just had to do without it. I carried thermos bottles full of scalding water to the horse barn to thaw out the water floats. I remember the temperature was below zero, but it was clear and still. We had a real bitter cold spell late in 1988, but I don't know if it was at the turn of the year. It might have been on into '89.

I've been thinking about some of the old weather sayings I've heard. We always mark down the day that it thunders in February, because it will come a cold spell and probably freeze on that corresponding day in April. Sometimes it doesn't thunder in February, though. The first norther in August will mark a good day for frost in November. I remember writing down a first norther that came one summer on July 26, but it didn't get cold on October 26 like I thought it would.

Here are some well-known weather proverbs: If the winter starts with dry northers, it will be a dry year. If the sun goes down behind a bank of clouds on Wednesday, it will rain before Sunday. If the ants are real busy, it may rain. Turner Harvey used to say, "Wherever you see a coach whip today you'll see water tomorrow."

If the flies or wasps are real bad, the weather is fixing to change. Horses running to the house may also signal a weather change. If the chimney smoke hovers close to the ground, it's going to rain. If the coyotes howl after daylight, the weather will change. If the moon changes on Saturday, it will rain. If the new moon comes when the wind is out of the east, a wet month will follow.

I had always heard that if it rained on Easter Sunday (Why do we always say that? Easter is always on Sunday!) it will rain seven days in a row. It didn't turn out to be true, though--I saw it rain on Easter one time and I thought it never would rain again. I've also heard that rain starting before seven in the morning will be gone by eleven, and that if birds get out in the rain it's going to quit raining soon. Usually when the wind blows day after day we think a rain is coming. That's often true, but I can't make up my mind—is the wind going to blow until it rains, or is it just not going to rain until the wind stops blowing?

Supposedly if snow stays on the ground more than three days, it will snow again. The longer it stays after three days, the heavier the next snowfall will be. If the snakes are crawling a lot, it will rain in about ten days. Ring around the moon, rain soon, and on and on. Mama used to tell me that Granddaddy Rudd always said, "Big fluffy June clouds don't move, they're just there."

Lots of times it seems like it rains when we wish it wouldn't (boy, that's been awhile, hasn't it?) like when we've just washed the car, or we wanted to go on a picnic or to a ballgame. You hear people joking about doing those things so maybe it will rain. I guess when it's as dry as it has been lately I'd have to say if you wash your pickup, tractor, or your wife's car, cut the hay down, start painting the house or take the shingles off and it still doesn't rain, it's time to get a real job.

. . . .

P.S. Last Friday I was telling one of my friends what I learned a long time ago from my friend Mr. West. He believed that the sun shines every Saturday, even if it's just for a few minutes. He admitted that there might be a Saturday or two in a five-year period when it wouldn't happen, but that's about all. And I haven't often seen it fail. In February of 1978 we had twenty-two days without sun, but it did shine all four Saturdays. Frances reminded me last Saturday night of what I'd said. "You told L. W. yesterday that the sun shines every Saturday, but it didn't shine today." I'd already been thinking about that. "I know," I said, "and I'd better tell him I was wrong. He probably already knows it, though." And then I thought, "As long as I was going to be wrong, why didn't I tell him, "It won't ever come a six-inch rain on Saturday?"

Photos

A dispute between brothers.

Gina (Boss Cow) and baby.

Big John, Faylene and Betty Ann. It takes them all.

Cattle and Trail Herds

Trail Drives

I'VE BEEN READING some before-the-War history that was written way back when, in the Deep South. It's about folks who lived, survived and multiplied in the wilderness or the big woods. Apparently the swamps, rivers, hills, mountains, and plains had a whole nest of such clans every so often. Y'reckon? Yeah, I do. And I'm here to tell you, these people were not a "standard thread", as we say in the shop business. They were woodsy, clannish, strange, or, as the old folks used to say, "funny-turned".

The book where I'm finding all this is *Cracker Culture: Celtic Ways in the Old South*, by Grady McWhiney, and it was printed by The University of Alabama Press. The rank and order of the different groups of such folks is not known to many, but I actually did know it from previous reading (see how much advanced knowledge I have? It's so practical and useful). It goes like this: Redneck, then Peckerwood and then Cracker. It seems as if the Crackers, along with their families and friends of like cloth, would drive their cattle to market. This might be a two-or-three day drive with some of the drovers on horseback and some on foot and all of them accompanied by lots of dogs. They would have to camp at night and guard the herd. Sometimes they would drive hogs. I can hardly imagine even trying to do that. I think they took ALL the dogs on one of these ventures. Sometimes the cattle or hogs were loaded on a barge and moved a long way down the river. Of course sometimes horses were driven to market, but if they were broke they could be tied together and led.

The earliest records of trail drives as we know of them here in the real cow country were left by a Franciscan missionary, Father Vasconcelos, who spent fourteen years in the Spanish province of Texas. His diary was discovered in 1971 by Father Benedict Leutenegger and was microfilmed for the Old Spanish Missions Historical Research Library in San Antonio. This diary is a wealth of information. In it Vasconcelos told of a drove of cattle leaving Zacatecas in Mexico for the Texas missions on October 13, 1777, with Father Jose Maria Camarena along as a missionary. Then on March 24, 1778, Vasconcelos again noted in the journal, "The animals of the missions of Texas arrived after 5 months and 11 days on the road." The "conductor" of the trail drive, Fray Jose Antonio Garcia, had ridden into San Antonio the day before. He had only four days to enjoy the amenities of the small frontier community before leaving for the long trip back to the interior of Mexico. He was back there by April 15, his trip having taken only eighteen days. On July 16, 1792, Father Garcia was relieved of his work as procurator and conductor for the missions. His successor, Father Vicente Parra, left Zacatecas on October 13 of that year with the drove of animals and supplies for the missions of Texas, but because of his inexperience and the bad weather he encountered it took him longer to make the trip. He did not return to Zacatecas until April 15, 1793.

There were many hazards connected with the frontier cattle industry. According to the diary left by Father Vasconcelos, in the first half of 1781 in his province, sixteen people were killed by the Comanche. Six of this number were soldiers bringing forage to the horses at the missions. Two men were killed while taking the hide of a cow. A man and his son were killed as they were rounding up their cattle. Times and conditions back then were hard, real hard as compared with the way things are now.

Texas Drovers

FIFTY OR MORE Spanish missions in the Southwest were abandoned years before the Civil War. Y'reckon? Yeah, I do, since so much recorded history tells about it. With no one at the missions to tend them, cattle and horses were left to run wild and multiply. Then many of the cattlemen went off to the War in which many of them were killed, and after it was over some of them relocated. All this left many Texas longhorns unattended and free to reproduce and become wilder during the years from 1861-1865. It was estimated that right after the War longhorn cattle outnumbered people ten to one. These cattle were there for the taking, or, literally, for the catching and branding. They were wild as buck deer and usually roamed about in small bunches. Enterprising drovers began to gather them in herds so that they could be driven to market, and this was done in a variety of ways. They were roped, caught with dogs, driven into pens, and trapped at night. If the cattle were not marked or branded, whoever branded them could claim them. What has always been on my mind was what a monumental chore this would have been, and guess what? In order to trail or sell them, you would have to catch them a second time!

At first there was a market in Louisiana and the Gulf Coast for these herds of cattle, but it was soon saturated. It became necessary to go farther to markets in St. Louis, Chicago, and, in a few instances, to New York. The only way for this to be practical was to drive herds of about two thousand head at a time. At first, mixed herds of cows, calves, heifers, steers and bulls were driven. Later on this was sometimes done if they were going far north or northwest to stock a ranch with cattle. Most of the herds were sold for beef to the government to feed people on reservations. Of course some was sold to beef suppliers, and all of these herds would be steers. Steers were also more manageable after they were trail-broken.

Trail breaking a herd was a long and constant procedure for the first few days. A herd was usually "put together" at a certain area that had adequate grass and water. They were watched day and night by men on horseback riding around them. After they had settled some, the drovers would start off early one morning by letting them graze off in the direction that they were going, and that's how the drive would begin. There would be twelve or fifteen men making up a trail-herd crew. The trail boss was paid one hundred dollars a month, the cook fifty. The cook's helper and the horse wrangler were each paid twenty-five dollars a month. These last two were usually kids, young kids. One case I know of from a local family's history tells of the horse wrangler being only eleven years old! The cowboys had their positions on the herd, from point men, side men, and then the ones riding the "drag", or tail end. On some of the crews these positions were permanent, while some rotated them since the drag could be so dusty.

Each crew had a chuck wagon driven by the cook and a hoodlum wagon for bedrolls, extra water barrels, etc., driven by the cook's helper. They probably had eight or ten mules they rotated to pull the wagons. Each cowboy had five or six horses which, along with the mules, made up a herd of about a hundred. They would have one gentle horse for a "bell horse" that maybe the horse wrangler could find in the morning dark to bring the remuda, or herd, in. They usually had a "possum belly" tarp that hung down under the bottom of the chuck wagon to carry wood when they went through a barren stretch.

The "chuck" to feed the crew was mostly beef, beans, biscuits, potatoes, syrup and coffee. Sometimes the cook might have some canned tomatoes to help make a stew or some canned or dried fruit for a cobbler. There would be salt, pepper, lard, flour, some sugar and, once in a while, cinnamon. The cook and his supplies for cooking were the key to putting together and keeping a good bunch of trail hands.

On the Trail

PREPARING TO GO on a trail drive was right smart of a chore. Y'reckon? Yeah, it was, and it took a long time, too. All of the cattle had to be caught and counted. In cases where several different people brought cattle to be driven to market, they were branded with each owner's brand and then branded again with one trail-herd brand on all of them. To rope and brand a herd of two thousand head would take a long time. These cattle were usually just held on a gathering and branding ground.

All of the horses had to be put in one place, maybe a rope corral, and then five or six horses assigned to each cowboy. The cowboys had to shoe all of them and get them to where they could be ridden. Each cowboy needed at least one horse he could rope cattle from and that he could depend on if the weather conditions were bad or whatever. He also needed a night horse, since all of the trail hands took turns riding around the herd at night. I think it was common for these horses to be pretty "bronky", as Daddy used to say, at first or maybe for a long time, but by the end of the trail drive they probably had all the kinks out of them.

The cook and his helper had to check the wagons, grease the wheels, and repair and oil the harness. Then all the supplies had to be bought and stored in the wagon along with all the pots and pans for cooking. The hoodlum wagon had to be loaded with horse-shoeing and harness repair stuff, along with the bedrolls. The herd had to be allowed to settle and work out some of their differences and maybe get the biggest part of the fighting over with.

Finally, early some morning the wagons would head out followed by the loose horses and cattle. They would probably make about ten miles a day. After four or five days, if there was a big creek or river nearby with good grass they might stop for a couple of days because some of the cattle and horses might be getting sore-footed and need a rest. If they got sore-footed again the drivers would try to sell them to a farmer or rancher or just have to leave them and go on.

The trail, of course, was fraught with all sorts of disaster. There were always rattlesnakes, some bad river crossings, deep or swift water and maybe water moccasins. Sometimes cattle would stampede at night when first on the trail, during a storm, or if they were aroused by rustlers or Indians. If this got started it could spoil a herd, causing them to get in the habit of stampeding. If this ever started, nearly all the trail hands would have to be up and riding around the herd all night. The popular saying of trail bosses was, "You can sleep when we get to market." The trail boss might have to pay to cross reservation land or to water a herd at someone's farm or ranch. These herds all eventually went to Dodge City or on farther north because they had to stay west of a quarantine line that ran generally south to north starting over in Louisiana.

So many accidents happened with stampedes, river crossings, Indians, irate settlers, rustlers and bad horses that many trail drivers died and were buried beside the trail. Most of them were young, but after all this was a young man's game. The trail boss himself might not be but twenty-five years old.

Some days on the drive were just long, hot and completely uneventful. It was a great day when they finally got the cattle to market and sold. Sometimes they would sell some of the horses, too, or they might bring them all back. A few of the cowboys later on might get to come back on a train part of the way bringing horses, wagons and all. Oftentimes when they got back they would find another herd waiting to be driven to market, or they might have to put a herd together.

The Goodnight-Loving Trail

ONE OF THE most heavily-traveled cattle trails was the Goodnight-Loving Trail. Y'reckon? Yeah, I do. According to history books, tens of thousands of cattle went up that trail, usually in bunches of 1500-2500 head at a time. The accounts of the two men this trail is named for, Charles Goodnight and Oliver Loving, are really interesting. Charles Goodnight was born in Illinois in 1836 and came to Texas when he was ten years old with his mother and stepfather. He rode bareback on a bald-faced mare. He worked on farms till he was twenty years old and then started his own cattle business. He belonged to a local militia to fight against Comanche raiders, joined the Texas Rangers in 1852, and was in the Confederacy.

Oliver Loving was born in Kentucky in 1812. He came to East Texas in 1845 where he farmed and ranched and also had a small shipping business. He too was in the Confederacy and was forty-nine years old when the War started. He sold cattle to the Confederacy during the War. He had led many successful cattle drives before and during the War to Louisiana, Illinois and Denver, Colorado.

When Goodnight came home from the War his cattle had multiplied greatly and he needed a market for them. He attempted a drive from his place in Young County north through Oklahoma and on up, but Indian raids, rustlers and all sorts of bad luck caused Goodnight finally to reach a point where he could give up on that drive, sell what cattle he had left, and return home. He was strong-willed, though, and soon started putting together a smaller herd to take on a different route. As he was preparing to leave with this herd, it happened that Oliver Loving came by with a herd and stopped to camp close by. The two men met and started talking about their trail-drive plans. It became apparent to Goodnight that he needed the help and knowledge of Loving, who was twenty-four years older and had led successful trail drives. Here a friendship and partnership was formed.

The two men put their herds together and drove them southwest from Fort Belknap to Fort Chadbourne. From there they had a ninety-mile trail with no water until they reached the Pecos River. This route was part of the Butterfield Stage Route and was referred to as being below the Comanche line. They started at night and drove the cattle three nights and two days. Along the way many cattle dropped out or turned back to the last watering place. From the Pecos they drove on to Fort Sumner, New Mexico, where the army had ten to twelve thousand Navajo and Mescalaro Apache to feed. Goodnight and Loving sold all their steers for eight cents a pound, then Loving went on north with the cows and calves. Goodnight went back home taking three or four of the trail hands with him so he could put together another herd. This time it would be all steers, since that seemed to be a better market. Loving and the other trail hands came back and joined the new herd not long after the drive got started.

After they got on the ninety-mile dry stretch to the Pecos, Oliver Loving and a one-armed trail hand named Bill Wilson rode way ahead to scout the country. A Comanche war party found them when they were four or five miles east of the Pecos. After a running battle, Loving and Wilson made it to the Pecos and up under a sandy bank washout kinda like a shallow cave. The battle went on all day. The Comanche tried to throw burning brush from the top of the cave back in to where Loving and Wilson were. They also tried to tunnel in from the back. The Comanche finally conveyed in broken Spanish that they wanted to talk. Loving walked out and was talking to the leader when another Comanche shot him with an arrow. The arrow went through his wrist and into his side. Loving made it back to the cave and safety. That night he persuaded Wilson to go for help. During the night Wilson, leaving behind with Loving his clothes and all of their guns, went into the water of the Pecos and got away. Finally the next night Loving also left the cave and was found two days later at a wagon crossing in the Pecos. He was taken to Fort Sumner where there was a doctor and army hospital.

In the meantime, Wilson walked three nights and rested two days going in the direction of the herd he knew was coming his way. He found part of a teepee pole to use as a cane, but was barefoot and hungry as well as thirsty and delusional. He said wolves followed him and would gather round whenever he lay down. He finally got to where he knew the herd would pass by and hid in a cave until they came. After he was rescued and by the time he, Goodnight and the others got to Fort Sumner to find Loving, the wound in Loving's side had healed but his arm was infected. He died at Fort Sumner on September 25, 1867. Goodnight took him in a wagon pulled by six mules and accompanied by two or three trail hands back to Weatherford, Texas, to be buried, as Loving had requested.

After Loving died, Goodnight continued his trail drives and moved from ten to twelve thousand cattle a year until 1875, when fences, settlers and railroads made it impractical. An interesting story about Goodnight and the drives tells of his lead steer, "Ole Blue", that wore a brass bell and led herds up the trail for eight years. Blue would come back from the drive with the saddle horses and mules. Goodnight said Ole Blue would never bed down with the other cattle, but slept closer to the horses as if he were some sort of royalty. Ole Blue lived for twenty years, and after he died Goodnight mounted his horns and hung them in his office.

• •

P.S. Parts of the book and movie *Lonesome Dove* are loosely based on Goodnight and Loving, with Goodnight of course being Woodrow F. Call and Loving being Gus. And another thing---Nolan County's own Darren Stevens is a descendant of Oliver Loving. I don't know that he's been up the trail, but he does move a lot of cattle with a big pickup and a trailer as long as a dry-land well rope---think about it!

Goodnight

NO, I'M NOT saying, "Good night." It's three p.m. and even I don't go to bed that early. I'm referring to Charles Goodnight, the man for whom the Goodnight-Loving Trail is named. He was a trail driver and took many herds of cattle to market, but that's not all he's remembered for. Y'reckon? Yeah, I do. He was also a ranger, Civil War veteran, inventor, farmer, college founder, conservationist, builder, businessman and movie producer. You didn't know that one, I'll bet! Another thing you might not know is that during his trail-driving days Goodnight got to thinking there must be a better way to keep food and cooking supplies and prepare meals while they were on the trail. He rebuilt and equipped an army-surplus Studebaker wagon for this purpose, and that's where the chuck wagon was born.

After the death of his cattle-driving partner Oliver Loving, Goodnight joined up with John Chisholm and their drives extended the Goodnight-Loving Trail so that it eventually went on up to Wyoming. Then in 1876 Goodnight and another partner, John Adair, founded what was to become the JA Ranch in Palo Duro Canyon. This ranch covered nearly a million acres and ran a hundred thousand head of cattle and a protected herd of buffalo. In 1878, Goodnight took the first herd of JA cattle out of Palo Duro Canyon north to Dodge City. A while later, when hungry Comanche came down from Indian Territory to hunt now-scarce buffalo, Goodnight made a treaty with Quanah Parker. Goodnight promised Quanah two beeves every other day if he would promise not to hunt the JA buffalo.

In 1879 Goodnight moved farther east on Turkey Creek to be closer to the railroad and built a log home where he lived with his wife Molly, a former school teacher. The 1880's were bad times for cattlemen in that area because of rustlers. Goodnight felt that he wasn't getting much help from law-enforcement officers and, typically, decided to find his own solution to the problem. He joined with other ranchers to form the Panhandle Stockman's Association with headquarters in Mobeetie, Texas. These cattlemen started taking care of the rustling problem themselves.

In 1889 Goodnight ended his association with Adair. He bought his own ranch and established the town of Goodnight, Texas. His ranch was the first in the Panhandle to have barbed-wire fences. Goodnight wasn't just a rancher, though. He was also a banker and newspaper man, and when he saw a need for higher education he established Goodnight College in Armstrong County. He agreed that he would build the college building, buy the supplies, pay the teacher and put in a well and windmill for water. All the teacher had to do was keep the windmill working and pumping water into the trough. There were always a lot of stories about Goodnight that ended with, "You wouldn't have wanted to be there," and one of those stories was about the time when Goodnight and his men rode up to the school to water their horses. Unfortunately for the teacher, they found the trough dry and the windmill not pumping. I don't know if we can imagine what followed.

Goodnight did something else that made him different from most ranchers and trail drivers. In the 1920's, he decided to make some movies. Of course they took place on his ranch and included horses, cattle, buffalo and Comanche hunters. He went too far with his endeavors, though, when he decided to invest in Mexican silver mines. The investment went bad and ruined Goodnight financially. He sold out to his friend W. J. McAlister in 1919, but the agreement let Charles and Molly stay in their home for the rest of their lives. Molly died in 1926, and Charles followed her three years later in 1929.

$\mathcal{P}.\mathcal{S}.$ Loneliness was a way of life for many ranch women. Molly Goodnight, alone for weeks at a time, looked forward to their cowboys coming by. When they did, she cooked for them. One of them once brought her some live chickens from Lord knows where. She kept them as pets, and in her own words and her own hand wrote her sister to say, "You've no idea how much company a chicken can be."

The Olive Bunch and Other Real Characters

MANY OF THE families of hard-grown cowmen were tougher than a boot full of barbed wire. Y'reckon? Yeah, I do! And they were often known to employ men that were rougher than a stucco bathtub. One such bunch was the Olive family--a mother, father and four sons from down near Austin. It was believed "Old Man" Olive had come from the South. The oldest son and leader was called Print, and he was followed in order by Ira, Marion and Bob. They were all highly volatile and, as the old guys used to say, "fractious". They were also hard-working, hard-riding and hard-pressing trail drivers who drove lots of cattle all the way to the South Loop River in Western Nebraska. They found that Nebraska had a shortage of horses, and in one year they drove several herds of them north until they had put seven thousand there.

Print Olive got into trouble in Nebraska and was kept in jail there until he could be tried for murder. It seems that his brother Bob, who had been appointed cattle inspector, was killed by two men he caught butchering cattle. The sheriff arrested the two cattle thieves, but Print and company wanted to take care of the matter themselves. They caught up with the murderers, and after the smoke had cleared and the funeral was over, the law indicted Print and tried him for murder. He spent a year "working for the state", as they say, and then was set free. Out of jail, Print was still a real rounder. When he caught a man skinning one of his steers, he didn't kill him, not really. He just tied the thief up real good, rolled him up in the hide, tied it around him, left him in the hot sun and rode off. Print himself was killed in Trail City, Colorado, in 1886 over a ten-dollar livery bill a cowboy owed him.

Other members of the Olive family were to be reckoned with, too. During the time Print was in jail, his brother Ira was the head trail boss. One morning Ira got into an altercation with a man named Leon over the handling of some cattle. Leon drew a knife out of his boot to throw, and when Ira saw that he drew his gun and shot Leon dead. End of altercation. End of story.

Another man of note during trail-driving times was Boise Ikard. He was a recently-freed slave who came to Texas with a medical doctor. Ikard was born with an infallible sense of direction, was fearless and extremely loyal, and knew a lot more about doctoring than most folks. Goodnight and Loving would always give him all the money to carry when they headed to a bank. That says a lot.

Clay Allison, another of Goodnight and Loving's drivers, was the subject of lots of stories. He had only spent a few months in the Confederacy when he was discharged for reasons described as follows: "Emotional or physical excitement or alcohol produces a condition that seems to be partly maniacal. This may have been caused by a blow to the head several years ago that left a depression in the skull." He was discharged from the Tennessee Light Artillery but still wanted to fight, so he joined the Ninth Tennessee Cavalry. It was said that in normal circumstances he seemed quite placid. O-o-o-kay, as the kids say. Allison was with Nathan Bedford Forrest and was captured in April of 1865, a month before the War ended (if, in fact, it ever has!) and was scheduled to be shot for being a spy. The night before his execution was to take place, however, he killed a guard and escaped. Soon after, the War was declared over. A little while later, he was at home on the farm with his brother and sister when an Illinois Cavalry corporal came to take all their possessions. Clay killed him, and he and his family moved west of the Brazos. He was fresh from all this when he joined the trail drive. He was twenty-six years old then and went on to become an infamous bad guy and gun hand. Let's review some of the stories about him, starting with the mildest:

At a visit to the dentist, Allison got up from the chair, looked in a mirror, and saw that the dentist had pulled the wrong tooth. He knocked the dentist down, sat on him, and pulled out two of his front teeth. And it was said that Bartholomew "Bat" Masterson, a Dodge City lawman, suddenly remembered another town he needed to go to when he got word that Clay was on the way.

After several killings and two acquittals, Clay started ranching and was trying to live a somewhat normal life. But before long, as was normal for him, he got into a round with another rancher over who had the water rights that lay between their ranches. The other rancher got really mad and challenged Clay to a duel (so-o-o-o sad!). Clay declared that they would dig a big pit and each of them would jump into opposite ends of it with a Bowie knife. Whoever died in the pit would lie as he fell and be covered up right there. Right then. Guess who got the water rights? Allison died July 3, 1887, in New Mexico. He was then a rancher, forty-six years old, and it was believed that he had killed fifteen men after his war days. Oh! And after all this, how did he die? He was going from town back to his ranch when he fell off the wagon seat and the back wheel ran over his neck.

Referring to the men and times of the trail drives, E. C. "Teddy Blue" Abbott, wrote in his book *We Pointed Them North* of being interviewed by a lady from a newspaper who politely asked, "I guess you boys had fun riding your ponies?" He responded in his easy way, "There weren't any boys and ponies, Ma'am. They were all men and horses."

Earlier I told the story of Molly Goodnight and how quiet and often lonely her life on their isolated ranch must have been. I couldn't help thinking of that after I read about the time the brothers of Print Olive were planning to break him out of jail. His wife begged them not to--she was afraid if they did he would be branded an outlaw. She might have been glad to have some of the quiet and uneventful life of Mrs. Goodnight!

He Rode With Goodnight

RECENTLY I FOUND out that one of Nolan County's own rode with Colonel Charles Goodnight. Y'reckon? Yeah, I do, as a matter of certain certified fact. It was W. H. Boyd, who settled on Bitter Creek in 1881. One busy day a woman came into my office, and when I asked if I could help her she said, "Go ahead with your business. I just came by to talk about history." She told me her name was Jean Boyd and that her grandfather-in-law had ridden back from Fort Sumner, New Mexico, with Goodnight when he was bringing his partner Oliver Loving home to Texas for burial in Weatherford. I was all ears. She came back later and left copies of a Midland newspaper account of the trip. It had been written by a Mr. Haley in January of 1932.

According to the article, W. H. Boyd was born August 5, 1848, in Missouri. His widowed mother moved her family to Texas, where they lived in Ellis and Dallas Counties during the War. She then married Mr. B. P. Merrell. They moved to Cook County in 1866, taking a bunch of cattle with them. The government was feeding over seven thousand Indians at Fort Sumner and was buying beef, lots of beef. John Chisholm began driving herds to New Mexico in 1866 and took two more herds in 1867. Goodnight and Loving left with their herd in 1867, and that was when Loving was shot by an Indian and later died at Fort Sumner.

At about the same time a drover named Bill Cloud left for New Mexico with eight hundred four-year-old steers, two wagons and twenty-four men to help him. The youngest of these trail drivers was nineteen-year-old W. H. Boyd. He remembered it as quite an adventure. They drove through Camp Cooper and Belknap, by Fort Phantom Hill through Mountain Pass in Taylor County. They went along the lower end of Mulberry Canyon and along the Butterfield mail route. At Camp Wilson, later Fort Griffin, they got an escort of six Union soldiers to go with them as far as Fort Chadbourne. From there eighteen men went as far as Horsehead Crossing on the Pecos.

The trip was far from easy. They ran into a storm of grasshoppers that came down like hail. They saw many graves along the way that were so new they didn't even look like they had been rained on. They saw one grave near Fort Phantom with a nearly new saddle on it and one on the Plains with a board at the head and a note telling the man's name and that he had been killed by Indians. They made it, though--in November of 1867 they turned the cattle over to a Mr. Rheams. He hired W. H. Boyd and six more men to stay with the herd, since the buyers just took one hundred head every third day.

About the time all this was over, Goodnight and his men left Fort Sumner for Weatherford, taking Oliver Loving to bury him there. There were fourteen men in this bunch, including W. H. Boyd. Goodnight had two freight wagons pulled by six mules each. They took Loving in one wagon and in the other one were provisions, including bedrolls, coffee, flour, bacon and enough corn for each horse or mule to have one quart a day. The return trip was much easier. They rode through herds of buffalo most of the way, the biggest bunches being where Winters is today. They covered about a hundred miles every three days. It took twenty-four days to get back, a distance of about eight hundred miles. W. H. Boyd died in Sweetwater on May 23, 1935.

•••

P. S. Mr. Boyd remembered that during the time they were being escorted by Union soldiers they met up with another bunch of drivers. This group, of the rough-and-tough, hard-to-bluff vintage, asked who the soldiers were. When they were told "Them's Yankee soldiers," their response was to laugh and say, "Well, I'll be. And here we thought they'd have horns!"

Help With Farming

The Soil Conservation

PRESIDENT FRANKLIN D. Roosevelt once came to the Texas Panhandle. Y'reckon? Yeah, he did. It was in July of 1935 when he got off the train in Amarillo. He had established a program named "Operation Dust Bowl" to try to save land that had been almost destroyed by the dust storms and by grasshoppers that had come like a plague and eaten everything in sight in spite of all efforts to destroy them. Fields had been set on fire trying to kill them, and in places big rollers were pulled over the fields to crush them, but there were hundreds of millions of them. This left the land at the mercy of the dry winds. In places it was blowing away at the rate of several tons per acre, leaving only bare sterile ground. The topsoil blew until something caused it to pile up. Some sand dunes in New Mexico were reported to be ten feet high. Something had to be done somehow.

When Roosevelt got off the train he was greeted by a big band, a huge flag and a hundred thousand people. A man named Bennett had presented the president with a plan that was actually the start of the Soil Conservation program, and his plan had gone into operation on April 17 of that year. Various agencies had been formed to implement it. In parts of Oklahoma, Texas and Kansas workers with the CCC, one of these agencies, had put out forty million tree saplings in rows in an attempt to keep the land stable. One program paid farmers a stipend to sign up their land to plant grass along these tree lines. This first plan took in about a million acres.

This "dirty decade", as it came to be called, caused one family in three to move away from their homes and land, leaving nearly ten million acres with no farmer at all. The government bought over eleven million acres and returned it to grassland. They established several national grassland areas. Some of the land never healed or became fertile again. Before the tree-planting move was over, two hundred million trees had been planted. After the wet years came back, some farmers bulldozed the trees out so they could have more wheat ground to plant. Some of the trees died of age or more extended droughts during the 50's, mid-70's or in the early 2000's, but some of them are still there. I have personally seen a few short rows of giant elm or cottonwood trees.

Much has been accomplished with the setting out of trees, contour farming in rows, planting of native grasses and of course irrigation. The latest move toward establishing grassland has been through the Conservation Reserve Program that we've had since the 1980's. We've learned a lot, but I'm sure we'll still make some mistakes as we try to move forward and progress.

Future Farmers of America

BELONGING TO FUTURE Farmers of America was a big high-school deal for all the country boys and, to our utter amazement, to some of the town boys as well. We learned all kinds of things and some of it stuck, believe it or not. I was talking the other day about how I keep records on everything and always have and someone said, "I'll bet you learned that in FFA." He was right---that is when I started. I remember learning that George Washington kept good records, so I guess all the partly-filled notebooks I have filed away are on account of old George. I keep records on my cows, and a while back I was having to pick out some of them to sell since it was so dry. I decided on a cow that I thought was one of my least desirable ones, but when I looked at her record I realized she had made more money than most of the others. Without records I guess I wouldn't know whether I was washing or hanging out. In FFA we could go to stock shows here in town and even to the ones in Abilene. That was so much fun. We got to miss school and also got to stay in a tourist court close to the fair grounds for two dollars each per night. I'm sure none of our mothers would have thought of letting us stay there if they could have seen it, but after all we were way off from home and so big and so free. Thinking back on those tourist courts now, I imagine they should have been burned down, pushed up in a pile and hauled off.

Another thing in high school that was really fun was the Big Red Marching Band. One year we won the right, along with five other bands in the state, to play and march in the Cotton Bowl at half time on New Year's Day. That's big stuff, period. It instilled in me the love of music that grows each year as I get older. Music is calming, it's healing, it's wonderful.

After the first excitement of cars and hotrods began to wear off, a bunch of us turned to being dyed-in-the-wool, honest-to-goodness, totally dedicated cowboys! I mean, it was like the song now that says, "I wanna be a cowboy, learn to ride and rope like Gene and Roy!" We would've gone to bed with our spurs on if we could've gotten by with it. We loved the whole thing. We'd brush our horses, trim their hooves, roach their manes all except a foretop and handhold on their withers, pull their tails, clean their saddles, plait halter ropes and bull ropes, and build bucking chutes and roping pens. We'd buy new grass ropes and keep them in prized clean lard cans, break horses, and get thoroughly discouraged trying to learn to rope off of half-broke horses. There was the joy of having mares and colts, and of even now still having horses. As a friend of mine said the other day—direct quote—"It's real dry but I wouldn't want to don't have a cow or a horse."

Somewhere in this time it got to be the thing to camp out and fish, and then to follow the coon dogs on Sweetwater Creek one cold wet winter. I think now my bunch had wide and varied extra-curricular activities. That doesn't seem so long ago, but it was. I sometimes think some of the kids now may be missing a lot

What you learn in school can have long-range effects. I know. When I was a senior I took a class in General Metals where we had a broad sampling of shop work with sheet metal, machine work and welding. One of my friends liked machine work and learned enough in that class to work in it the rest of his working life. I decided I wanted to learn how to weld and still remember that when I started they thought I already knew how. Big whoop! No, not really. Being able to burn a rod does not make you a welder any more than being able to drive a nail makes you a carpenter, being able to saw a board off square makes you a cabinet maker, or putting a new end on an extension cord makes you an electrician. Along that line, I've told a few young men that if they wanted to be successful and didn't mind working they should find a trade they had a knack for. And then I'd tell them, "Try to learn it from the best people you can find. The rest is simple. Just show up on time or before, do what you said you would do, and charge what you said you would charge, or even less. You can have a hundred-dollar job and charge ninety-five for it, and that five dollars you didn't charge will get you more good advertising than the whole hundred dollars would buy."

Last night I dreamed I was talking to two government men who were taking some sort of general survey. They were well-dressed, educated and polite. They asked me, "If you could say one thing to be put in the results of this survey, what would it be?" I said, "Don't ever underestimate the value of a good public school education."

. . . .

P.S. Being a person of habit, I go to the barn every morning by the same route and pass the home of a guy I've known forever (nearly). He has all these signs on his property---the usual stuff, such as No Smoking, Beware of the Dog, etc. One day I thought, "None of them say, 'Don't honk'!" So for a long time I've been honking every day. I was sure he didn't know who it was, but then one day when I honked Donald was sitting out on the porch grinning like no one else in the world can and he waved at me. I guess now he knows.

This is about me.

— Dad —
— Dru —

Tool Boxes

YOU KNOW, PEOPLE say things like, "I can tell you a lot about that woman by the purse she carries." Y'reckon? Yeah, they do, and it's true. I know I can. It may be a purse, or what someone drives, what sort of boots he wears, or any of a long list of other things that reveal a great deal about a person.

I'm not much of a mechanic at all, but I admire those that do have that kind of mind. Some of these folks have large, neat tool boxes that, with tools included, probably cost as much as a good pickup. They are, understandably, usually real protective and territorial about those toolboxes. And it's no wonder, as they can all tell you of a special wrench that was borrowed and never returned. Or, sometimes it can get worse, with stories of the ones who borrowed it, loaned it to someone else, lost it, or had it get stolen with all their tools. The worst scenario is the one where they can't remember ever even having it.

This is all strange in a way, because most people know you don't mess around a kitchen with a cook's "stuff". Maybe that's because of chuck wagon cooks in the western movies. But they may not realize this possessive and territorial streak also goes with cabinetmakers, carpenters, tile installers, electricians, plumbers, welders (hello) and anyone in the trades. I guess two of the most un-Christian like fits I have ever had came about when someone "borrowed" something off my welding truck, didn't put it back, and I didn't miss it until I was thirty miles from town in the middle of the night and had to have it. I stuck a welding truck in mud plumb up to the spring hangers, so I

106

jumped out, ran around to the off side and stepped up by the headache rack to get my shovel. It was gone! Not there! What now?

Of course, not all toolboxes are neat or organized. Some mechanics have tools scattered all over everywhere, up on top of things, in the floor, in or on a toolbox, in the seat or on the dash of their pickup. And then some of them have real neat toolboxes or carry-around toolboxes that they just set in the pickup when they go out on a call. This is all under about the same theory as messy desk versus neat desk. As you probably know, a messy desk or art studio is sometimes thought to show more creativity.

All in all, I think toolboxes on pickups just about tell it all. Mine has various kinds of pliers, crescent wrenches, vise grips, hammers, water trough floats, nails, fence staples, ear tags, tree pruners and saws, chains, jacks, ropes, axes and pinch bars. And don't forget oil, soap and WD-40. You see a toolbox like this and think, "stock farmer". I saw a tool box the other day with paint brushes and rollers, caulking, light bulbs, plumbing parts and fuses. I thought, "rent house owner". A toolbox with whips, walking canes, ear tags, ropes and rubber boots says, "cattle buyer".

One more real-life story: One time Delbert Biers, a really good mechanic, was working on something for me. I found a little something I could do myself while I waited, so I asked Delbert if I could borrow a crescent wrench. He said, "Real mechanics don't have crescent wrenches, young man."

••

P.S. Well, I guess it's hog-killing time. The dishrag was frozen in the sink this morning.

Hands

WHEN I USE the term "hands", I'm not talking about extensions of our arms. Y'reckon? No, I mean employee-type hands. When you hear people who employ workmen talk of "hands", you can pretty much bet it's something to do with skilled or unskilled labor. One of the funniest things I've ever heard along this line was something a woman told me a few years back. I'd stopped by their place of "bidness", as we say here in our part of the country where "the earth am flat and the sun do move." It was one of those places where hard unskilled labor went on every day from early to way past late. The woman in the office was telling me how far behind they were and how she hadn't had any luck hiring extra help. She added that just that very morning her husband had said, "We need some hands," just like she hadn't been looking for some, so she told him, "Well, you're just going to have to look out on the end of them arms!"

I can think of a lot of real good hands that we have had back in the oil field days. Probably the best one ever was Bud Green, who in 1947 had opened the shop that we bought from him. Bud and his wife Mattie stayed at the shop for a few weeks until we got started, and then Bud came back to the shop after he got all his fishing trips over with. He just wanted to go back to work, and did work part-time for a few years. He was absolutely unbelievable. You cannot imagine what all he could do and what all he knew. He'd started welding in the early Thirties making ten cents an hour and having to work sixty hours to get on overtime. He said they used to drive to Hamlin to work on the

108

boilers at the gins, but didn't get paid for riding up there or back to Sweetwater. And then when they got back to the shop he worked out of, he had to walk home. Every time he bought new bib overalls he would tell me how much they cost and then say, "When I first started welding, overalls cost fifty-seven cents." Later on he told me he'd seen some high school girls wearing right new-looking bib overalls with the "lags" cut off. I don't think he ever got over that! I remember when his brother-in-law lost so much weight on a diet that he had to buy new overalls, so he sent all his outgrown ones to Bud. They were just a fit for him at forty by twenty-eight inches.

Bud wouldn't waste much time talking when he was working, but would talk a lot if we were driving a long way to a job. If he talked long enough, he'd always tell about someone he'd known along the way who was really good. I'd think, "Here I am riding with the best all-around shop man I know, and he's talking about somebody that was good!" He told me one time about asking an old man how he knew so much and the old man said, "Well, Bud, I started in nineteen hundred and twenty-two." I asked Bud to tell me a story about that man. He thought about it and then said, "Well, one morning he came in the shop with a thin china saucer and I asked him what he was going to do with it. He said, 'Well, the widder woman next door wants to hang it up on her wall, so I'm going to drill a hole in it,' and he did."

Bud told me he always saved all of his overtime money so they could start their own shop, and it was surprising how fast it added up. He said "Why, it wasn't but about fourteen years until we had enough." I never saw a man that Bud didn't like, and I never saw a man that didn't like Bud. He could be real funny and had a great sense of humor that few people ever saw. He also was a well-disguised politician who could get along with anybody. One time he asked a young man working there at the shop, "Was you supposed to have been twins?" The boy answered, "No. Why?" Bud said, "Well I just never did see no one feller that thought he knew so much."

One time Sweetwater was frozen over solid, right about the turn of the year. All the motel rooms were rented and some people were doubled up in rooms. The Ranch House Motel was full and the boiler was out, so they had no heat or hot water. Bud and I went out there and put all fifty-two boiler flues in new. This probably should have been a two-or-three-day job. The ice was so bad it was hard to get around, so I took my lunch and Mattie brought Bud's lunch. He had three fried-egg, bacon, lettuce, and tomato sandwiches on toasted bread, a container of pickles, olives, peppers and onions, a piece of cake that was really about three pieces, a big piece of pie, a thermos of tea, one of coffee, and one of cornbread and milk. I watched in total amazement as he ate all of this and then said, "I used to eat hearty when I worked all the time."

One night late at the shop we were doing some real heavy welding and I kept turning my machine up and Joe Garcia, a real good young welder that Bud had raised (taught), was turning his down. Finally we figured out we were in such a mess we had our leads crossed. At times like these, as unlikely as it seems for Bud, he would say, "Let's stop, turn everything off, put all the tools away and clean up the shop. We have such a mess we're wasting time." We would do all of this and then start over, and it really would help.

One time Bud was working way out in the shop yard when some little dogs got his gloves and took them up on the porch of the house north of the shop. Bud hollered and said, "Mattie, go over there and get my gloves." She said, "Go over there and get them yourself. I'm busy!" Bud said, "I ain't going up on that woman's porch while her husband's gone off to work!" Mattie went and got'em.

Bud could do an unbelievable amount of work, and Mattie could keep the office, do all of the billing, ordering and paying. She also knew how things should be built or fixed. Contrary to all the tales you may have always heard, Mattie Green did not weld, could not weld and, like she told me one-on-one in the shop office one day, "Why, I wouldn't dare learn to weld. Don't you think I have all I can do?" I said, "Yes Ma'am, but I'd always heard you could weld." She said she thought maybe that got started one day when Bud told her to hold his welding hood and lead while he got under a truck and some roustabouts drove up and saw her. She wasn't about to tell anyone she couldn't weld. That's some more of that political stuff I mentioned. They were both really, really good business people and neither of them was about to tell anyone something contrary to what that person believed. Sometimes Bud would joke and say, "Boy, that's a mess. We may have to let Mattie do it." Let me tell something else that might surprise you: When push came to shove, Bud was the undisputed boss. Bud and Mattie are both gone now, and may the Lord rest their souls. No better two people ever lived.

Proverbs 22:29
> Do you see a man skilled in his work?
> He will serve before kings
> He will not serve before obscure men.

Young Hands

I HAVE FROM time to time had some outstanding young employees. Y'reckon? Yeah, I have. James Payne, a long-time friend of mine, was the welding instructor out at our very own Texas State Technical College. I learned a lot from him. He had been a "real world" oilfield welder, and moved here to teach at the college. He really does know about all phases of welding. I've always called him Mr. Payne, as I first did when I was going to night classes out there. He usually calls me "Blackie Crow" or just "Blackie", but that's a whole 'nother story. Yeah, I know, I've got a bunch of them. As a matter of fact, I have so many stories I don't ever have to make one up. Someone once asked me about attending a fiction-writers' class and I just said, "Why?"

Anyway, Mr. Payne would call from time to time and tell me he had a student in need of a job who was really probably all right--green, but willing and anxious to learn. He never did send me a bad one. I want to tell you about some of them and assure you that I'm not saying any of them are better than the others. A "best welder" would encompass way too much stuff. If someone asked me about a "best cook", I'd have to ask, "Campfire, kitchen, breakfast, meat, chicken, fish, desserts, bread or what?" It's the same way with welders and anything else in the trades. As I wrote before, "You can teach a chimpanzee to drive a nail, but can he build your cabinets for you?"

The last young welder I had comes to mind first. His name was Scott Walker and he was from Bangs or Early, I never can remember which. He was well-mannered and clean, the top two of my requirements. He also had a good attitude. Scott told me he was learning to weld, but didn't know about anything much. The first clue I had that he would be good came when we went to get my pickup where I had left it to be fixed. I told him what had been done to it, and he said, "I could've done that!" I was surprised. "You told me you couldn't do any mechanic work." To which he replied, "Oh, I just don't want to overhaul one or anything."

After that day, Scott took over such jobs as they came up, and I never did find anything he couldn't do. He could run a winch truck or tractor, work by himself, anything. One time we were working in Aspermont and I decided to get through with the job because we'd been up there long enough. We got through about dark. I told him to take my welding truck home and I'd follow him in Armbruster, our winch truck. He got out to the edge of the yard and stopped, waiting to make sure I got started and going. I commented on this when we got home as being something that just the old hands knew to do. He said, "Oh, no, you have to wait to see if everybody has got started and going, and you have to be real certain that they're not just rolling off." I thought, "Real Hand!" I finally asked Scott one day why he knew so much and what all he'd done. He said he had started out when he was twelve working for his granddaddy, who had roustabout trucks, a dozer, a maintainer, backhoe, pulling units, a water-well rig and some farm equipment. No wonder!

Randy Frizzell, another of the best young hands I remember, was one of the hardest working and most decent young men I ever had. He really didn't know how strong he was. Once in a while he'd pick up my torch and use it, and after he'd turned it off I'd nearly have to get the big pliers to turn it back on. Randy was always real time-conscious and felt pretty urgent about getting jobs done. He was a good welder early on, and also had something of a mechanical mind. That was really needed. He could do any kind of farm work, and one Saturday we were sprigging in Coastal Bermuda Grass. Sprigging machines are extra heavy. We pulled the one we had to the farm with a pickup and used it with a tractor. When we went to unhook the pin, it was bent in a real U shape and wouldn't come out of the drawbar hole. We had to saw it out with hacksaw blades. Yes, just blades, finally! I had three or four blades and we wore out or broke them all. Randy said, "Stan, I put those broken hack-saw blade pieces in the toolbox on Zsa Zsa (my tractor). I figured with the messes we get into we might need them sometime." I thought, "Real Hand!"

That's just two of many, so let me finish by telling about one I didn't hire. This boy's mother, a real nice lady I knew from her job, called me and said, "I was wondering if you might hire my son. He's eighteen, and has had welding in high school." I thought, "Oh, boy! Your son can drive nails, so you think I can send him to build a house." But I tried to be easy about it. "No, Ma'am," I told her, "You have to have a lot of experience to work full time out of this shop." She kept on. "You could take him with you and teach him." I said, "No, Ma'am, I've taught in public schools, but I was the one getting paid, not the students, and I don't have any work contracts that allow me to have a paid helper." She wasn't ready to give up. "You could send him to do the easy stuff." I said, "Okay, picture this. I send him to a lease to weld on a cattle guard, since that's not hard to do. The pumper comes on the lease and finds a gas leak. And naturally he thinks, 'Oh, boy, there's a welder up at the cattle guard. I'll get him to fix this leak.' Y'reckon! Really, now, is this a real welder who can do such a dangerous job as that?" The poor lady kept trying so hard I felt sorry for her, so I told her as nicely as I could, "Ma'am, we have to be able to get up anytime of the night, go no-telling-where to do no-telling-what, find our way there, do the job, get back without going to sleep and be back to work the next day, unless we're still gone. We're kinda, sorta, like the Texas Rangers--we go one in a bunch!"

••

P.S. The early bird gets the worm, but the second mouse gets the cheese.

All-Around Hands

THINKING ABOUT GOOD hands or capable employees, or individuals with varied talents, I remember a lot of them. Y'reckon? Yeah, I do. The subject here is folks who can "get'er done," as they say now. When such folks go to do something, they won't come back and say things like, "That was the wrong key for that lock," or, "The tractor wouldn't start," or, "It had a flat." No, no! They go to do it, and that's the way it's going to be. Getting in over their heads is just not on their screen. Remember the movie called *The Big Country*, where Burl Ives played the daddy of a bunch of boys that were "real citizens"? One day the boys came back from an altercation over a water hole, and Pa said, "How come y'all ain't dead, coming back here and my cows ain't watered?" Pa was expecting all-around hands, not "buts" and excuses.

The first all-around hand that comes to mind is Monk Boyd. One time he was going out to our farm at Palava to do some dozer work. About half a mile before he got there, his hauling truck blew a radiator hose and lost all its water. Monk got to thinking about an old Ford car that some of our renters had abandoned at the farmhouse, so he walked down there, took a hose off that old car, and walked back to his truck. He trimmed the hose to fit on his truck and then used his water can to fill the radiator. He drove on to the field, unloaded his dozer and went to work. When I heard that, I thought, "All Around Hand!" Please understand, this is just one of many such stories about Monk.

I guess without a doubt the most out-and-out, all-around oilfield hand I ever worked around is Amos Roberts. I have built some stuff for him at my shop while he was telling me how he had it figured out. After I'd get through with whatever it was, I'd ask, "Amos, you reckon this will work?" And he'd say, "Oh, it's got to!" And it would.

Back when I was a kid working at the lumberyard, I used to haul lumber to Lester Batteas. Lester's wife Frances would help him, and together they could build a whole house. Please hear that. I said "whole house", and I don't mean "except" anything. I'm talking about building a house all the way from foundation footings to chimney cap.

I just talked to a friend from Scurry County named Billy Ray. He told me he was building a wagon wheel out of mesquite wood, and then he said he guessed he'd finally found something he could do. Now, I've known Billy Ray a long time, and I thought he could do anything! I know he can harness a team. Oh, you can too? Well, that's good, but he's got the wagon for them to pull.

One thing I've noticed about all-around hands is that they'll always show you something out of their toolboxes, and then tell you there's a story that goes with whatever it is. It will be something like, "See this funny-looking little wrench? Well, it got me and Wilbert Dean home one night!" The wrench probably isn't big enough for them to have ridden it like a witch's broom, so you do have to wonder. Here's a story and an example of the way we talk: "Yeah, we took that load of hay up to that 'ranch' (a large expanse of land), and on the way back the filter in the face of the carburetor stopped up so we took this 'ranch' (mechanic's tool), got the filter and 'renched' (flushed with fluid) it out, and came on in."

When some of us were fixing to graduate from Sam Houston State College with degrees in Industrial Arts, Mr. Snodgrass, a professor I'd done some work for and who really did know just about everything, told us this story: Back in World War II, our Country Campus Farm had been a prisoner-of-war camp. German prisoners of war had been brought there, and they'd requested and received certain kinds of saws, files and woodworking tools, as well as certain kinds of wood which they used to build and finish grandfather-clock cases. Next, they wanted some different saws, files, and metal tools and certain kinds of metal, from which they made and installed the clockworks. The finished clocks ran and kept perfect time.

When the story was finished, we all just sat there big-eyed and silent for a minute. And then Mr. Snodgrass finished by saying, "So, when you boys get out there teaching or working in the trades, and get to thinking you're good . . . ."

I'd like to mention two young men who are well on their way to becoming top all-around hands. One is my son-in-law Joe Rivas, and the other is Brian Barns. I'm proud of them both.

. . . .

P. S. Quote from one of my old all-around hands: "When you boys get to thinking you're indispensable, go stick your finger in a bucket of water and then pull it out. Did it leave a hole?"

Photos

Half-sisters Gretchen, Ursula, Gisela and Gretel.

One big guard cow with horns for every bunch.

Sorrel geldings, two brothers plus one.

Schools and Teaching

The Hook Man

REMEMBER THE HOOK Man story? You know, the one that made the rounds when we were kids, or at least some of us were? It went something like this:

"Oh my gosh, y'all listen. You are not going to believe this. It is like soooo scary! Durrell Wayne and Gwenna Fay were parking out by Lake Sweetwater and they kept hearing this scratching around the car, they thought. When it got so bad that they knew they heard scratching, Durrell Wayne finally got his old '52 Ford started after nearly flooding it and they drove back to town as fast as they possibly could. They parked at Starr's Drive-in, plumb up by the building where the carhops come out. Ruby Nell, one of the carhops on duty, came out and took their order—his was black coffee (he thought that's what James Dean would have ordered) and hers was a cherry lime coke. Ruby Nell returned with their order and put the tray on the window—she always, I mean always, had to tell Durrell Wayne to roll the window up a little. (Wouldn't he ever learn? I mean really, now.) As she turned to walk off, she said, 'What's this hook hanging here on the door handle?' Gwenna Fay gasped and turned white. 'Oh, no, we knew something was terribly wrong when we heard that noise. And to think we never did believe our older cousins about the Hook Man that lived at the lake! Oh no, oh no, please don't let Mama hear this or she won't ever let me out of the house again!' "

Absolute true story, we knew some kids that knew them. (Not the kids themselves, of course, but just some others who'd heard about it.) Y'reckon? Yeah, right.

Now we live with modern day Hook Man stories. You haven't heard any, you say? Oh, yeah, I bet you have. Try this one that's been around for years. One of my own cousins from out of town came by several years ago, a while after his mother, who was my aunt, had died. He sat in my real estate office and told me, "Yeah, I know we agreed that Mother's house should just bring ten or twelve thousand, but I've been talking to this guy and he told me a big company is fixing to move a hundred families in here and people will be paying more than that for a chicken house to live in." So he waited, and then waited awhile longer. And while he was waiting, the deterioration, taxes and insurance kept going on until he finally sold the house for about what we had figured to start with, but it was three years later. Hook Man story alert!

One more, then I'll quit. It seems everybody has heard of somebody who is "just too smart." What? You never heard that about anybody? Well, supposedly, what being "too smart" does is cause people to act "different", or to be "funny-turned." I've heard people say a person was just "too smart when he was a kid, and it did something to his brain and left him acting dumb." Hook Man story alert! Or the ultimate oxymoron: "He's so smart he's dumb." Yeah, right! Y'reckon? Really, now!

Teachers

ONE OF THE very most important professions in our society today is the teaching profession. Y'Reckon? No, I don't just reckon, I know it is. Think about it with me. Early in their young lives, we entrust our small children to kindergarten teachers, who are in reality standing in for their mothers. It is of utmost importance that these little ones get started off right. That's why these teachers are highly educated, with years of training and preparation. They spend so much of their time as young adults, not to mention a great deal of money for college, getting ready. And I guess on top of the money spent, they could theoretically add on how much money they could have been making if they'd taken jobs right out of high school instead of attending college. My wife Frances is a retired teacher, our older daughter Holly is a second-grade teacher, our younger daughter Alison is a middle-school choral director, and her husband Jamey is working on a Ph.D. in school psychology. I myself have a few years' teaching experience and realize that as a teacher you touch people's lives and direct them in ways that will last from then on.

Alison and Jamey will be here this weekend. I know what will happen, as it usually does, and I'm looking forward to it. Frances, Holly, Alison and Jamey will end up sitting around our table and the subject will be children, and ideas about how to help them, or how to improve their own teaching methods. I'm allowed to sit and listen if I don't interrupt them. I can raise my hand if I need to ask something. I sit there and think, "Here at this table we have nearly forty years of teaching experience, not counting mine, and more than twenty years of college education represented." Then I realize that all of this is concentrated on methods of teaching, or on the individual needs of one student at a time. And to top it all off, it's Saturday or Sunday, and these people are supposed to be off for the weekend! Would anyone even venture a real wild guess at what the tab would be if you had four people of any other profession concentrating on a child or one situation on a weekend day or night? There won't be any charge for the benefits to the students of these teachers, though. After all, everybody knows teachers are way overpaid anyway, and have all that time off.

I have always felt privileged to be able to sit in on these sessions and also sad to think that a five-minute look at this would totally astound and amaze so many people. And the real sad part of it is that so many of them would be parents.

More Teachers

MOST FOLKS REMEMBER their early school years and their first few teachers for a long time. Y'Reckon? Yeah, they seem to. Anytime you get a group of people started talking about school, you'll hear lots of stories about those times. I started first grade in the fall of 1947 and missed going to school at Palava by four years. The school there had closed after the first six weeks in the fall of 1943 when it was consolidated with Sweetwater. I know this was a sad day, and it began the downhill slide for the community. For a long time, the old school building was still used for community events such as plays and a Halloween Carnival and a few things like that. The cotton gin stayed open another ten years and closed after an extremely short run for that ginning season. The church probably lasted about fifteen years after the gin was gone.

When I started to school, the addition being built onto East Ward School (Philip Nolan) was not complete, so the first graders went to class in the basement of the Methodist Church. We took our lunch and everything was new and so exciting. Mrs. Jones was our teacher and we learned how to print our first names and how to read from Dick and Jane. Later we graduated to another book about them, called Fun with our Friends. Mrs. Jones taught us on the blackboard how to play softball, and then we went outside and played. Up beside the teacher's desk was a glorified playpen with a big printed sign on it that said, "The Pig Pen". Any time you didn't do right, guess what? Yeah, you guessed it---you got put in that pen. One Friday we got new readers so we could take them home and read the first story. On Monday, it became obvious to Mrs. Jones that this one little girl and I hadn't done our reading. I will never forget how upset our teacher was. Well, we got put in the pigpen and it was a terribly sad thing and so embarrassing. I told this at our class reunion last year and the girl that was sentenced with me plays like she doesn't remember it. I kinda understand, because it was a traumatic thing.

In the second grade, my teacher was Miss Bennett. We all just thought she was the greatest teacher because she read us a real book with chapters. She would read a few pages of it every day after lunch. Miss Bennett is the teacher I've talked about before, the one who was gone to the office when we had our big Crayola fight. We had someone watching for her to come back down the hall, but we were well into the fight only to discover she had gone out the front of the office and all the way around the building and was watching us from outside the windows. Lord, deliver us, please, we were absolutely scared to death. We lived through it, though, and went on to the third grade where Mrs. Dulaney was our teacher. She was a really good teacher and an exceptionally kind person.

In fourth grade I was in Mrs. Faver's class. It was her first year to teach that grade, and there were forty-five of us in the class. We had desks with book racks in the bottom, and we nearly had to turn sideways to get down the aisle between the rows because the desks were crowded so close together. Down one side of the room were metal lockers that would all open when the first one was opened. There was a bookshelf on the east wall, and that's when I read my first book that wasn't a textbook. It was about Alexander Hamilton. Maybe that's why I'm still such a history buff and reader. We had only one big jar of finger paint, and it was black. I didn't even know finger paint came in colors until I had kids of my own.

Fourth grade was the year we learned borrowing in arithmetic. I still remember Mrs. Faver's way of explaining it to us—she said it was like going to the number next door and borrowing a cup of sugar. We'd have to remember to pay it back. I also remember that up above the blackboard in that room was a paddle that looked like it had been made by cutting a small tennis racket shape out of a two by twelve board. It had holes drilled in it, and we thought they were for the blood to squirt out through when you got hit with it. Mrs. Faver had us all believing that she had eyes in the back of her head and could see us even when she was writing on the board. Now she sits on the back row at church, and I sometimes catch myself looking at the back of her head if I happen to pass behind her.

Oh Lord, if some people just knew what we remember of the things we learned when we were young!

Minnie's Diary

SOME PEOPLE HAD a real hard time getting started on their college education. Y'reckon? Yeah, I do. One of them was Minnie Fry. She was from hereabouts and graduated from Newman High School in 1928. In reading her diary, I was struck by the vast amount of difference in going to college then and going now.

Let me tell you what I learned from following Minnie through her first week away from home. On a day in January, she and her friend Elsie George left Sweetwater headed for Abilene. They didn't have any money or anyplace to stay, but were determined to go enroll in Simmons University. They walked around Abilene all day until they wore the taps off their shoes. At six o'clock that night they still didn't have a place to stay or anything to eat. Then Elsie thought about a cousin who was living in Clyde, so they phoned him and he came to get them. He took them home to his mother and daddy's house in Clyde where they stayed overnight. The next morning at 6:30, Minnie and Elsie left Clyde and got to Abilene at 7:30. Again they walked around town all day until they wore holes in their hose and made their feet so sore it was hard to button their shoes.

Finally the two girls found a room to rent and then went to the college to register. In a typical first registration day, they were sent here, there, yonder and everywhere, but finally did get registered. Some of their classes were Education, English and Bible. The dean wanted them to stay in the girls' hall, but they were determined to do better than its rate of twenty-two dollars a month since they had borrowed their school money in the first place and wanted it to go as far as possible. They went to bed early that night, having had nothing to eat but an apple apiece all day. Their landlady let them use her bedclothes until they could get some of their own.

Without eating breakfast, the girls reported to their first classes the next morning as freshmen in Simmons University. They got back to their room at 12:30, and after resting awhile they went to a small Piggly Wiggly store and bought a few groceries. They walked back home and fried some Irish potatoes with their little bit of lard. They put some red beans on to cook and scorched them four times, not being used to a gas stove.

The next morning they slept late, and after eating eggs and bacon they left the dishes and rushed off to class. On the way, Minnie discovered she still had her house slippers on and had to run back and change. They waited a long time in the classroom before discovering that the class only met three days a week and that wasn't one of them. They did go to other classes at 3:30 and 4:30, then Minnie went to the library to study and Elsie went to downtown Abilene for the first time. She had walked halfway to town before she caught a bus, and then she walked all two miles back to save the ten-cent bus fare. In town, she'd bought four onions for four cents. That night the girls ate beans, onions and fried cornbread for supper and then went to bed.

On Friday, Minnie and Elsie went to classes and to the library to study. They were expecting a package from home, and when they got back to their room, sure enough it was there. They tore the package open expecting food, but instead found bed linens and a smaller parcel containing a large piece of lye soap. They ate supper and went to bed, but listened to the radio until 12:00. The last song before the station went off was "Home Sweet Home", which didn't help the two homesick girls a bit.

On Saturday, the girls spent some time in the library and went to their only class of the day, which was Bible. They cleaned their room for the first time since living there, then got ready to go home for the weekend. They left Abilene in a Ford touring car at 2:30 and got to Sweetwater at 5:00. Minnie's family lived out near Lake Trammel, so her sister and brother came into town to get her and took her home. And so ended the first week.

More from Minnie's Diary

THE WAY THINGS were when Minnie was in college was a lot different than it is now. Y'reckon? Yeah, I do. After Minnie had spent the first week in Abilene at Simmons, she went home south of Sweetwater for the weekend. On Saturday evening her beau came to get her and they went to the telephone office in town where his sister worked. Minnie got home at one o'clock and went to bed. When she got up Sunday morning she didn't even eat breakfast, since she'd been eating so little during her week at college that she'd lost her appetite.

Her cousin came that morning in his new Chevrolet coupe and took Minnie to church and Sunday school at Calvary, which was a church built on land that the Fry family had donated. There was a big dinner at the church, but Minnie still wasn't hungry so she just went home and ate a little bit. The family had gone to Sweetwater and bought some fruit, so after church that night Minnie ate fruit for supper.

On Monday morning, Minnie got up at 6:00 and left Sweetwater at 9:30 with her daddy and youngest sister all crammed into a Ford coupe with a lot of canned goods in the trunk. They got to Abilene at 11:30 and found that Minnie's roommate Elsie had red beans cooked and ready for them to eat.

The next day, after going to class and the library, Minnie and Elsie walked for twenty-five minutes to get to the Walnut Street Meeting so they could hear Jack Winslett preach. Afterward they walked back home and got there at 10:00. Minnie explained that they just could not spend the twenty cents it took to ride the bus.

Another day, the girls decided after class to cook butter beans, but never having done it before didn't realize how much the beans would swell as they cooked. The pan, the only one they had, got full, so they put some of the beans over into a large sauté pan.

On a Saturday, Minnie and Elsie walked the two miles to town, then walked all around looking for the post office. They finally found it, and again walked a long way trying to find a street that would lead them back to Simmons. When they found a policeman to ask, he laughed and asked them why their mothers had let them out of the backyard.

The girls went to the grocery store one Saturday and came back to find a strong smell of gas in their room. They opened the windows and called Mr. Lee, the landlord, who came and tried to fix the gas leak. When he thought it was all right, he tested it with a match, which was a mistake. The whole side of the room caught fire. Mr. Lee ran and turned off the gas meter in front of the house. Minnie and Elsie grabbed their clothes off the wall and threw them in the floor, then started throwing buckets of water on the fire. When the fire was out, there was water all over everything and the paper was burned off the wall.

One time the girls went home for the weekend and came back to find Mrs. Lee moving all their things into another room because she had rented their room to someone else. They weren't very happy about that, so they found a woman who would let them live on her back porch that had been closed in. They paid her $42.50 a month and moved in on March 14, 1928.

The next semester, the girls came back to Abilene with Brother Tankersley and Brother Laurie to register for spring classes. They moved to Mrs. Henry Morgan's house at 2620 Pine Street on May 17, 1928. After spring finals on June 5th and 6[th,] they went home where they attended a wedding and then J.C. and Mable brought them back to Abilene to attend the summer term.

This diary of Minnie's was a good look at college life back in the 1920's. In the remainder of the diary, Minnie writes of coming home and her daddy taking her to town to buy some new work shoes. She tells of helping milk cows morning and night and working at Home Dairy Milk Plant. She tells of Jack coming to get her and going to L.D.'s filling station to put oil in the car. While they were there they got to listen to the prize fight between Jack and Mack over L.D.'s radio. On a Saturday night Jack came to get her and they went to town so he could get a haircut. The next day they went to Shannon Pool at Merkel.

Minnie went on to be a teacher, and taught at the Palava School when she was not much older than the students. In her class she had one of my daddy's brothers and one of my mother's brothers. She taught at several different schools in Nolan County, some of which are now gone but not forgotten.

Minnie married and became Minnie Cooper. She and her husband had a farm and nice home in the Champion area. She is remembered by many, not only as a good teacher, but also as an unusually generous and helpful person.

Training

THERE'S A PLACE in The Book where it says, "Train up a child in the way he should go, and when he is old he will return to it." Y'reckon? Yeah, I do. As a matter of fact, it's in the sixth verse of the twenty-second chapter of Proverbs. This training, or teaching or whatever you want to call it, goes on all our lives and involves all different kinds of trainers. Actually, the woods are full of trainers of all kinds. There are natural trainers, self-made trainers and even professionally-trained trainers. These folks teach people to work, play, get along and be more proficient in all manner of things. Of course, just because they really know their business doesn't mean they can successfully convey their knowledge to others, but that's not what we're talking about. And as a rule, the more training someone has, the more he's compensated for it, but that's not where this is going, either.

We all know about animal trainers for dogs, and horses, and on and on, but something that's so common and to me so unbelievable is the fact that humans sometimes don't realize the need for young humans to be trained as well. They do need it, though, and those who have caught on to this should also realize that it may never completely stop. Humans actually have to have more extensive training than any other species. For instance, some horses of good temperament and mind can be useful at an early age if they have a competent trainer. (I do mean horse trainer, not horse breaker. For instance, I myself have broken a few horses but I don't claim to be a horse trainer.) There's just so much to teach children from early on until maybe they're grown.

But when are they grown? It's absolutely staggering to think about all the instruction between potty training and college graduation. Just think about manners, driving, having jobs, having friends, having pets and helping around the house or farm.

Some parents, of course, miss some things. I guess we all miss something. Of course, some of the training doesn't take, or else maybe the kids rebel. Most people are taught (or not taught) to take care of things, to mind their own business, and on and on. All our lives most of us have heard things like, "My goodness, didn't your mother tell you not to tell someone what bad things were said about them?" Or, "Didn't your mother tell you not to ask personal questions?" Or, "Didn't your mother tell you it's rude to stare at people?"

Some of the kids showing up at the elementary schools today don't appear to have had much raising. It doesn't make any difference how good the school is, children need a good start at home or they may never catch up. I think originally schools were set up to teach the three R's, and most of the rest was the responsibility of the parents, but the teachers I know assure me this isn't true any more.

After your children reach a certain adult age, the teaching can turn around on you. With computers and all sorts of electronic gadgets we have now, as well as constantly-changing trends, parents are finding themselves on the other side of the training. For instance, a time or two Frances and I have told the girls about a certain movie we were going to watch only to hear, "Oh, no! Y'all can't watch that!"

East Ward

AFTER SPENDING THE first six weeks of school in the First Methodist Church basement, we in first grade felt really settled and thought we were old hands. Y'reckon? Yeah, I do. And then the addition to East Ward School was finished and we were sent over there. Boy, oh boy, what a major change that was. It looked like East Ward had about a jillion kids and some of them were giants. The fifth and sixth graders looked to us like all-star wrestlers. The big girls were so bossy and must have thought we were woefully ignorant. They were always telling us what to do, or more likely what not to do. Now, when lunchtime came we went to the cafeteria, and it was always packed. Only one school bus had come when we were at the church, but at the big school there was a whole fleet of them and they all looked just alike. Above and beyond all else, the school had an office and a PRINCIPAL with sharp teeth and horns who was ruler over all, even our teacher Mrs. Jones.

This was the year Mrs. Jones taught us to play baseball. She drew diagrams on the board to show us how to play before we went outside. The ones who were batting were "in town", while the ones who weren't batting were "in the field." There were three bases and a home plate. The catcher got to bat first when you came to town after the other team had struck out three times. All of that really stuck in my mind. One time in college I was living in a dorm and stopped in the lobby where my roommate and a bunch of other boys were watching the World Series on television. The team in the field came to town and when this guy got up to bat I asked why he was getting to bat, since the catcher was supposed to bat first. They got all big-eyed and out-of-breath and asked where I had gotten such an idea. After I told them that's what Mrs. Jones had taught us in first grade, things really went downhill.

This morning I was out in our front yard when the school bus came by. I had forgotten you can smell a school bus. Why can you smell a school bus? And why do they smell like that? Riding the school bus was a whole 'nother deal, let me tell you. That is the original survival of the fittest. The big kids, mean kids and tough kids sit in the back of the bus, and the little kids sit in the front if there's room and if they get there in time. There are volumes yet to be written about the ones of us who survived riding a school bus. I remember how kids used to get put off the bus for misbehaving. It usually didn't make any difference where the bus was, either. I remember one case of two boys getting put off the bus and starting off running across a field to take a shortcut home. They knew if they got home late their daddy would know they'd acted up and got put off the bus. And if that happened, there wouldn't be a time out or a spanking; it was going to be time for a whuppin'! A bad one, then and there, with no lengthy speeches to prepare them for it.

Another time on the bus a boy decided to light a Zippo lighter and hold it under the hair of the girl sitting in front of him just to see what would happen. The next thing we knew he was standing up slapping her on the head with both hands and she was screaming bloody murder because her hair was on fire. And once, as the bus was passing a man on a Farmall tractor out where the A T&T building is now, one of the big mean boys was chewing tobacco and spit a stream of tobacco juice out the bus window and hit the man on the tractor. The bus driver put the boy off right there, even though it was about eight miles to his house. And then he got really mad when the man on the tractor apparently felt sorry for the boy and picked him up.

The grade schools got out earlier in the afternoon than the high school, so we were just sent outside to the playground until the bus came from high school to take us home. That was a whole different education in itself. There was a faucet sticking out of the west side of the school building, but it had no handle on the stem. After we'd been out awhile and just about the time we thought we were dying of thirst we'd find two sticks to mash together on each side of the stem so we could turn the water on.

We spent most of our first school years in mortal fear of the initiation we were going to get from the sixth graders at the end of our fifth-grade year. But we were saved by a twist of fate when East Ridge School was built and some of us were sent over there for sixth grade. The powers that be decided those of us who lived on the bus route north of town would go to East Ridge. Among the mercifully-saved were George Hoover, Skipper Neeper, Wayland Smith, Jimmy Scott, Wendell Whittenburg, Glenn Imken and I. And some more, I'm sure. I don't remember any of us being too sympathetic with those left behind to face the initiation.

A Free Stick!

BACK IN THE days when we were big kids at East Ridge School, it seems like we ate a lot of Popsicles. I remember that it was always a big deal when you finished eating one to look and see if you had a free stick. Y'reckon? Yeah, I do. The story was that about every jillionth Popsicle was on a stick that had "free" printed on it. That meant you could return the stick to the Popsicle man and get a free Popsicle! That might have been just a kids' rumor, I don't know. It does seem like I did see a free stick one time, but I wouldn't swear to it. Anyway, we'd be out on the playground and someone would see a Popsicle stick on the ground and holler out real loud, "That may be a free stick!" Then the race and the scramble was on to try to be the one that got it.

I guess Popsicles really were a big thing, because I remember there were so many leftover sticks around that kids were making things out of them like little houses and, of all things, fans. These fans were made of sticks interwoven to make a square, with one sticking out for a handle. It sounds like a joke now to use something like that for a fan, but it just reminds me of how unbelievably hot it could be in those schoolrooms in the early fall and late spring. Late spring toward the end of the school year was trial enough for grade school kids and their teachers even without the heat. Air conditioning in schools (or anywhere else, for that matter) was unheard of, as were electric fountains with cold water. The fountains we had produced a stream of lukewarm water if they gave out any at all. (Where in the world do we get "lukewarm", of all things? Where did that come from?) So many times the water would shoot up real high and get all over the floor, while at other times barely any water would come out. This might be because someone was flushing a commode in a nearby restroom, which was always a wholesome and comforting thought!

At East Ridge all of a sudden we were big enough to play football, we thought. I never will forget all the excitement we had about naming our mascot. I remember campaigning for the name "Longhorns" (no, no, we had never even heard of a college, much less their mascot). I don't know what we became. There was a lot of talk about the "Hornets", and then all the excitement moved elsewhere when it was rumored that we were getting green jerseys. I had no idea what a jersey was and wouldn't ask, even though it was quite puzzling to me. The only jersey I knew anything about was a cow. We had one, but she wasn't green and I had never seen one that was. We did finally get our green sweatshirts and some pants, shoulder pads and helmets. We probably looked really nice, but we never won a game, ever. I don't think we ever even made a touchdown!

Then there was P. E. class, and basketball. There was always and forever and probably still is some kid that was double-wired and about half spider monkey who would be dribbling the ball and looking straight ahead. I would be ninety degrees to his right and looking at the moon when here he came with the ball and managed to hit me in the chest with it. I heard someone say they guessed I just wasn't athletic, like that was a sin that would condemn me. But I can say I like to play tennis, I can throw a rock and hit something and I can rope. So maybe that's some form of being athletic.

I guess out of all this what still stands out most is the time we must have spent looking for those free Popsicle sticks. There's no telling what all we missed or overlooked because of it. We just knew that if we looked long enough and hard enough we'd get something for nothing and it would make us a lot happier and make everybody else wish they could have been the one to find it. And now let's stop and think for a minute. How much time and hope do we still waste chasing free sticks?

144

P. S. We were in Stillwater, Oklahoma, last weekend where our grandbaby Ben lives. That meant we missed Sweetwater's biggest weekend of the year. I thought about what was going on at home and remembered a real funny Hee Haw scene. The Culhanes (remember?) were lined up on a bench and completely devoid of expression. Lulu asked, "Grandpa, remember when it came the great bananner storm?" Grandpa said, "I remember, and hit weren't the bananner storm that caused the ruckus. It was the thirty thousand monkeys that came to eat the bananners that weekend."

Junior High

BEFORE I GET started, it seems that a slight correction needs to be made in my last story. All the mania concerning "free sticks" happened at East Ward School, not East Ridge, where we had undoubtedly outgrown popsicles. My bad.

Sixth-grade rumors about Junior High while we were still at East Ridge were rampant. Y'reckon? Yeah, I do! We heard them all. All the sixth graders from the four elementary schools would be there in the seventh grade together. All four schools---that was awesome in itself! On top of all that, we who were now big sixth graders were fixing to be little seventh graders ruled by big eighth graders. Oh, such dread and apprehension! The very worst thing we had been told was that each of our classes would be in a different room with different teachers. And they had bells for each period, and tardy bells. If you couldn't get to your classroom and in your seat by the time the tardy bell rang you were in big trouble.

Well, after all our dread the day finally arrived. The morning was spent registering for classes, and then we got to go home. School didn't start then until September, so I spent the afternoon of the first day at a tank with more country kids, shotguns, and shells, shooting at dove. It's a real wonder some of us didn't get killed. (I'll save the nearly-got-shot story for later.) School started the next morning with no more time left, just bang! It started and kept on keeping on. So many books, so many kids, so many teachers.

146

By a great stroke of luck I got put in Mrs. Overton's English class. It was on the bottom floor, down and across from the office and easy to find. That first day I managed to get there and seated long before the tardy bell rang. Now, for the great-stroke-of-luck part. This girl came walking in and sat down near me. I took one look at her and thought, "I'm nearly twelve and a half years old, and where has this girl been all of my life?" I had never seen such a beautiful girl before. So of course I was thrilled beyond words after we were alphabetically seated and I sat across from her---Mary Frances Davis was her name. We laughed and talked and whispered and giggled until a few short days later Mrs. Overton lost patience and stood us out in the hall. I was on one side of the classroom door and Frances was on the other side by the girls' restroom. She saw the principal come out of his office and immediately ducked into the restroom. This left me holding the bag with the money, the horses and the shotgun. I was in trouble, big trouble, by myself! I thought, "Boy! These town girls here in the big school really play rough!"

One of the major dreads of the big school was a history teacher, Miss Wade! Miss Wade had started teaching early in life by passing a test that allowed her to teach right out of high school while continuing her education. She was absolutely renowned and had taught the parents of some of her students. She had even taught our principal, Thomas Whittenburg. She was a good teacher and was first on the list of those who ran a tight ship. I distinctly remember one day when Mr. Whittenburg happened to walk by our classroom for the third time. Miss Wade went out and stopped him, looked up at him, and said, "Thomas, you still have a seat in my class any time you want to know what's going on."

One big thing that had somehow escaped our preview of Junior High was that hall traffic went in one direction only to avoid congestion. Frances spent two whole years trying to see if she could go backward in the hall without Mr. Whittenburg catching her.

High School

GOING FROM EIGHTH grade in junior high to ninth grade at Newman High School was a big move for us. Y'reckon? Yeah, I do. By the way, I graduated from Newman High School, named after the family that gave the land. Some time after this, when a new school was built it became Sweetwater High School. I remember thinking and wondering about the change in the name. I just thought, "Did the appreciation of the Newman family giving the land for a school wear off, or what?"

With an amount of excitement and much apprehension, we entered our freshman year. This school was bigger and in several different buildings, and even the kids were bigger. Some of the juniors and seniors had gone to different elementary schools than ours and were too old to have been in junior high with us, so we never had known them. We were already used to different classrooms and teachers, but this school had a cafeteria that looked so big to us.

High school brought all kinds of exciting things new things like FFA and band that occasionally had meetings or practice at night, which was nearly more excitement than we could deal with. It was the time of first having drivers' licenses and of having cars to drive, of hair oil, Butch Wax, real Levi's worn real low with no belts, mambo shirts, taps on our shoes, going to forbidden places like the upstairs pool hall and Starr's Drive In, bebop records, Little Richard, Paul and Paula, Dion, The Four Tops, and Elvis with "You Ain't Nothin' but a Hound Dog." And don't forget Faron Young, Slim Willett,

Hank Snow, Johnny Horton, and Sonny James singing "Young Love". I had formerly said that one was by Marty Robbins until J.(just) T.(terrific) Petrie kindly corrected me. (Thanks, J. T.---my bad.) I won't ever forget the girls, either---Brenda Lee, Timi Yuro, The Dixie Cup Singers with "Going to the Chapel", and Sue Thompson with "Sad Movies" and "Norman". And there was going to midnight movies at the Texas Theatre to see Sandra Dee and boys with names like "Moon Doggie" in beach movies that we were sure were way beyond real cool, since most of us had never seen anything with more water than a red muddy tank. Or I guess some of the town kids had seen Sweetwater Lake.

At some point in time our cars became the be-all to end all. We washed them, waxed them, sanded them off until our fingers bled, and left primer spots on them until we decided what color they should be painted. We had the upholstery redone, took that old horrible unthinkable stock muffler off and put on one called a "smitty" that was real loud, or if we were really cool we'd put on dual mufflers or "pipes", as we called them. We were all real good mechanics because ninety-five per cent of the cars were six-cylinder Chevy's or flat-head Fords. We could put in points and plugs and maybe change the brushes in the generator, break a tire down to patch the tube and pump it back up with a spark-plug pump, so we knew everything! Kids---we get aggravated with them, but we were *really* kids!

• •

P. S. Some of the movies we saw were set in New York City and showed kids eating something called "pizza pie". Back then we had no idea what that was---can you imagine?

Going to College

I LEFT HOME one morning about 4:30 to go to Sam Houston State College in Huntsville and start on a bachelor's degree. John Kearney was going, too, but he was starting a master's. It seemed like we drove forever to get there. Y'reckon? Yeah, I do---it was three hundred and eighty-two miles. I don't remember that I had ever been that far from home before. When we got there we checked into a three-story dormitory named Jackson Hall---as in Andrew Jackson. I had never seen so many kids in my whole life, and they were from everywhere. We found a school cafeteria across the street and up on a hill, like so many things there are up on a hill. We later discovered this was one of three cafeterias on campus, plus a snack bar in the Student Union Building. Each class was in a different building on a large campus, and it was a blessing that our school catalogues had maps in them. I always had to walk to class because you couldn't park anywhere. Sam Houston was ahead of other schools at that time in that each dorm had suites---rooms in pairs with a bathroom in between, and every room had its own telephone.

My roommate was from Oakwood, a six-man football school a few miles north of Huntsville. His name was Charlie Ray Bing. The Lord never let a kid live that was any more of a kid than Charlie Ray. He was personality-plus, should have been on "Mayberry." He had dark skin and hair and had a fair-skinned blonde girlfriend named Paulette. They made a nice couple. She was from Buffalo, up the road north from Huntsville and nine miles west of Oakwood. At least twice a week I heard about Charlie Ray being the quarterback at Oakwood and Paulette being a cheerleader at Buffalo. They played every down of every game all over again. It included all of the, "What if Donnie Ray had caught that pass? etc." I mean, it turned into serious replays. Of course we all had our favorite hometown stories, but one that I especially remember Charlie Ray telling and enjoying so much was about an Oakwood patrolman they called Old Rip. If they could get Old Rip into the pool hall on Saturday night and get him talking they'd crowd around him so he couldn't see the main street out in front of the building, then some kid would go driving through town about seventy miles an hour and would honk as he passed the pool hall. Of course Old Rip would run to his patrol car and give chase. The kid he thought he was chasing wasn't there any more, though---a little way past the pool hall he'd slowed down, turned around and sneaked back up the alley and through the back door so he could be there when Rip came back from his futile chase. As Rip came in, some kid would say, "Did you catch'em, Rip?" And Rip's answer would be, "Yep, caught'em right before they got to the river. Gave'em a ticket and eat'em out real good. It'll be a long time before they come through here again!"

We had a serious card game going on in the dorm all the time. It was called "Sergeant Major", and I have no idea now how we played it. All I remember is that we had fun and Charlie Ray and I were always partners. There were pool tables in the Student Union Building and a big pool hall a couple of doors up the street from the dorm. "Town" began across the street from our dorm.

Sam Houston Park with some of Sam's old houses was behind our dorm. It's a real pretty park. It was maintained by prisoners watched over by a horseback guard carrying a shotgun. That was a sobering sight. There were some twins in our dorm who drove a convertible. They were first-class clowns of the Chris Farley type. One day right after lunch they drove by the prisoners working in the park. The twin riding on the right side leaned way out and yelled, "Run! We'll pick you up on the corner!" S-o-o-o sad. The law came from every direction while the horseback guard kept his shotgun trained on the boys. Law officers took them to the main prison, known as The Walls, in town and kept them until nearly midnight. They called the president of Sam Houston, the police station in the twins' hometown, and their poor mother and daddy, who probably weren't at all surprised!

So much fun, so many kids, so long ago. Frances and Paulette became friends and the four of us would go on picnics together and to the movies and such. We went to Buffalo and Oakwood with them sometimes and they came to Sweetwater with us. But then, as often happens when college is over, we went our different ways and after a few years pretty much lost contact. We were really happy, though, a few years ago when Charlie Ray and Paulette came by our house. Holly was home from college and kept looking at all of us and saying, "And y'all were in college together like my friends and I are now?" Paulette couldn't stop saying, "Holly looks just like Frances did." She didn't have any girls, and I thought she was going to take Holly with her. Alison wasn't home, but when Paulette saw her picture she said, "She looks just like Stanley did."

And then one day when I came home from the country Frances said, "A lady stopped at the office today and handed me this Buffalo paper and said Paulette had asked her to tell us that Charlie Ray died." It shocked us nearly to death! (To the lady who brought the paper: If you read this please call us.)

Frances and I were back on the Sam Houston campus in July of '04. Such a pretty place. Lots of trees, green grass, and orange and white flowers. Frances took my picture standing by a statue of Sam Houston in front of the old Education Building. I showed it to a friend of mine who commented on how pretty the building was. I said, "Yes, it really is. And it was built five years before the War. She asked which war I meant and I told her, "The Civil War."

....

P. S. Remember how I said we had never heard of pizza pie when we were in high school? Well, the first one I ever ate and enjoyed was one Frances made in her dorm room at Sam Houston from a Chef Boyardee mix. We took it to the park and shared it, and it was so good. And the memory of it still is.

Kids and Professors I Knew in College

AS WITH MOST things, remembering a little leads to remembering a lot, so I find myself thinking of more and more people I knew in college. One of my roommates was called Junior. He was a nice clean-cut intelligent boy who, like me, had never known much outside his upbringing in the Big Thicket. He was bashful about that, but after we'd known each other a few months he decided I might be pretty country too and began to feel at ease. He told me a few tales from the Big Woods and I didn't make fun or act like I didn't believe him, which led him to tell more stories that were real interesting. He belonged to an old established family with a lot of way-back history. For starters, they had Grandpa's trunk at home and it still had Confederate money in it. He told of people he knew who ground their own meal from corn they had raised themselves and who still lived mostly off the land. We talked about hunting, fishing, trapping, hogs and hog dogs.

Junior knew a lot of real good old stories that had been handed down, like one about a man who, during a trial in the courthouse, took a high sign from his brothers, jumped out of a second-story courthouse window, mounted a tied horse and made it back to the woods where he stayed . . . forever. And one about a family of brothers who, ten years after the War, had got cranked off on "shine" and started telling about their feats when they were the Grey fighting the Blue. They decided whoever was the bravest would go squat on a stump, crow like a rooster and let the others shoot at him . . . they buried him the next day. We talked about Woods things happening while we were in college, like the man who took his pet woodpecker and showed it to a professor who had recently published an article saying that kind of woodpecker was extinct. And the story of a log hauler who had recently lost a quarter in the jukebox in a bar. When the bartender refused to return the quarter, the hauler and his friends backed a winch truck up to the front corner window of the bar and threw the hook and line through the window. Then one of them went inside, picked up the hook and line and threw it out the side corner window. They hooked the line back into itself and pulled the whole building off the stumps it was resting on. I mean, they were hard-working men who took the loss of a quarter real seriously! Remember when Jerry Clowers told all those stories about the Ledbetter family, which included Marcel, Raydel and Aunt Pet? They were hilarious. One of the best ones was about a disgruntled pulp wood hauler who got mad in a bar and sawed up tables, chairs and even the bar. We'd all laugh till we cried, but I noticed Junior never laughed. Finally one day I asked him why and he said, "I've seen all that for real."

Another boy I got to know had grown up on the Texas-Louisiana line in a house that backed up to a swamp. He was always talking about going out the back door and getting into a boat to go somewhere. I couldn't even imagine such a thing. I mean, when you're from Fisher County and you think a red muddy tank is a lot of water, those stories were something else again!

Another of my roommates was a boxer. One time I went with him to Houston to see Cleveland Williams fight. Williams won that one and before long was on his way to the title fight, but then he made the mistake of trying to outrun a highway patrolman who shot him through one kidney. That ended his career. We also met and talked to Roy Harris, who was a real nice mild-mannered guy. (Yeah, you do--he was a heavyweight from Cut & Shoot, Texas, who fought Floyd Patterson for the title in 1954.) He was on the front of Life Magazine. It had a story about his family and the clans in the Big Thicket. But there's not enough room here for that . . .man!

Naturally I also had some interesting professors in college. One was my drafting teacher, who had a vast amount of knowledge. He owned a bunch of rent houses and I rented an apartment behind his house and worked for him. To this day I still use things I learned from him. He was highly intelligent and a hard worker with an Andy Griffith personality.

I had an English professor who loved to tell stories about ghosts, haunted houses, and things that happened in them. Another professor was a germ freak to the highest degree---or so it seemed. He had tape around his windows and waxed paper (that dates it, doesn't it?) taped over the ducts in his house to keep the germs out. But then he would go to the Student Union Building and buy a packaged sandwich, unwrap it and put it down on the table without a plate or a napkin or anything under it. I mean a table where kids piled books, tennis shoes and coats and played cards---go figure!

College for Fisher County farm boys is such an education. Y'reckon? Yeah, I do!

. . . .

P.S. One more note about high school FFA---Newman High School had an exceptional agriculture teacher who taught from education and experience and by example. He was a good teacher, good man and good guy . . . Mr. Frank Davis.

Horses and Dogs

Pee Wee

PEE WEE WAS all horse and he knew it, every day, without a shadow of a doubt. Y'reckon? Yeah, I do! Let me tell you about him. I was staying at Mama Johnson's house one winter Saturday when Daddy came late that evening to get me. He told Mama Johnson, "Stan and I are going to Fort Worth in the morning to get a horse that I found for him." That was a total surprise to me. Daddy told us that the horse was a two-year-old Shetland stallion. I was absolutely so excited that I could hardly stand it!

That was Daddy's way of announcing things. This is one of those good things that I learned way back then (I was eleven years old) that never has washed off. That's the way I am too, much to the puzzlement of some people. Allow me to show you a real life example of this. You have to stop by somebody's house and all their young'uns are in the floor bawling their eyes out. You think their dog has run away from home or no telling what. Upon inquiry you learn, "Well, their daddy told them last month that we were going to Six Flags today, but then he had to go to work and fill in for someone that had an emergency." Buffy looks blank for a minute when I try patiently to explain how I feel by saying, "Well, if you'd waited until last night to tell them instead of telling them a month ago they wouldn't be in the floor bawling, would they?" There's nothing criminally wrong with this type of scenario that I call "front running" except it causes problems oftentimes that would have been easy to avoid. Now what do you think Skip and Buffy will do with aforementioned young'uns when the other kids at school ask them about their trip to Six Flags?

Back to Daddy and the horse. He went on to explain that the horse was thirty-nine inches tall at the withers but since he was a two-year-old he would grow some until he was five. I guess Daddy said that for my benefit and not his mother's, since part of Papa Johnson's livelihood had been raising and training horses and mules. So many people don't understand about measuring from the withers. I sometimes am astonished at how tall someone is showing me their dog is until I realize they're showing me the height to the top of his head. Just think--when Pee Wee grew one more inch to reach forty inches he was ten hands high. It's common for horses to be sixteen hands now. That's just six hands or twenty-four inches taller than Pee Wee was, but let me tell you he didn't know it!

Daddy and I left for Fort Worth early the next morning driving a '49 Chevrolet pickup with Hobbs sideboards on it. When we got nearly to Fort Worth we turned left and went up north just a little ways to a barn. They had a big plank lot with a half dozen or so horses in it. And there Pee Wee was--as pretty as you can imagine. He was just like a real Quarterhorse but real small, with a thin neck and not very much mane. He really was a most unusual little horse---a Palomino, gray and white Paint. Daddy backed the pickup up to a chute where they loaded cattle so we could load him. Daddy knew a lot about horses and really did like a gray gelding that was there in the lot and thought about buying him too, but he decided he really didn't need him.

We took Pee Wee back home and I started riding him that very afternoon. They said he had never been ridden, but I guess some of their kids must have been riding him because I just saddled him up and rode him around the lot and he was okay.

Spot Hale lived on the Newman ranch and I used to go help him round up cows, I thought, but I was probably just in the way. Pee Wee really liked this too. He got to be around other horses and, after all, he was an "only horse" at home. We had a buggy that he would pull and he never did give any trouble about that either. A couple of different times Daddy took Pee Wee, the buggy, harness and me to town so

I could be in a parade. Pee Wee really was just a good-natured little horse. I roped off him, too, in the lot just to see how he would act. When I was playing Indian I would ride him bareback and carry my bow and arrow.

I had to have several horses after Pee Wee before I realized what a nice little horse he really was. I had a brown Shetland named Lightning that was a typical Shetland. Another one named Kickapoo was a gray stallion and was really just a little horse like Pee Wee. I've had several horses since I was eleven years old and never have been without a horse but one time, and that was just for a few months. We have three horses now. I remember all the horses we've had and some of them were really big, but I don't remember one that was a bit bigger than Pee Wee.

I Might Need Some Help

OH, MY! THE very wonder of knowledge, knowing, and understanding of dogs, cattle, horses and cats. If I open the bottom cabinet door below our pantry and take out a certain saddle blanket, our dogs Maggie Mae and Otis Lee start jumping up on the back door with all the excitement common to junior high cheerleaders. They know that's the blanket I put in the seat of my pickup Rufus so they can go with me to the country. Y'reckon? Yeah, they do. After I put the blanket in and go back to the utility room for the dogs' leashes, Frances and I have a routine that goes like this: Frances will say, "Do you need some help?" I always answer, "Well, I *might* need some help." Then I ask Maggie Mae and Otis Lee if they want to go help me, and of course by that time the jumping on the door and barking is nearly to the point of being frantic. I go out on the back porch with the leashes, and the dogs start trying to push each other out of the way, each one wanting to be first for a leash. When we finally get to the pickup after much tangling of leashes and going opposite ways around a carport post, I have to make them move over so I can get in and fasten my seatbelt.

Maggie Mae, a black and white three-year-old Jackrat, was the "first dog", and therefore her place is standing in my lap looking out the driver's side window. Seventeen-month-old Otis Lee, my Beagle, sits beside me until we get going, and then he'll lie down in the seat with his head butted up against my leg and take a nap. When we get to the country, Maggie Mae jumps right out and starts chasing whatever she sees first—birds, wasps, bees, flies or whatever. The other day, a water-float mishap had created a mud hole that looked like five hundred gallons of dark chocolate. Maggie Mae ran and jumped, and I *don't* mean just waded, right into the middle of the mess where it came halfway up her sides. But, after all, it had about two hundred wasps on it that needed catching! Otis Lee will immediately start sniffing and trailing all over everywhere. He'll sniff on a trail until he comes to a place where something has crossed it, and then he'll turn off and follow that trail until something else has crossed it, and on and on. The cows will see us and come up and I'll feed them some cake. The horses will come up from the other direction and get fed.

On the way back to town, Maggie Mae still doesn't miss anything, and Otis Lee gets some more rest. When we're home again, the dogs want a drink, and then Maggie Mae gets her ball and wants to play. Otis Lee has to sniff all over the yard to see what's gone on since we left. In the house, the air conditioner is on, the music is playing and the phones are ringing. But the cats Lee Roy, Palomino and Samantha are asleep on the back of the couch and on the settee to show us that none of it is bothering them.

Think about all this with me. When I wanted to go, the dogs were ready right then, without asking, "Where? How long? Who will we see? When will we be back? Can we stop by such and such a place? Can we call Lassie and Rin Tin Tin and King to see if they can go?" And when we got to the farm, the cows probably thought, "Wow! Cake!" and I didn't hear Bossy say, "Elsie, didn't you hear me order ranch? This is bleu cheese!" The horses said, "Oh, boy! A treat!" not, "I ordered thick crust, not thin!" And the cats didn't say anything, as if to ask, "Things bothering us? What things?"

I might need some help. We all might need some help! Hello, y'all—I think the dogs, cows, horses and cats have just provided it for us by example, if we would just settle down, straighten up, shape up and pay attention.

Photos

A long drought and then 14 inches of rain on Fisher County Road #127

Cows coming through the gate.

Fisher County pasture.

Miscellaneous

Other Folks' Businesses

WE ALL THINK from time to time that someone else's "bidness", as we here in the country say, is just ideal. "Y'reckon?" you say. Yeah, or at least I know I do. But normally when I hear someone talking like this I think, "You better not decide anything about that horse until you saddle him and ride him a while." Or, another one of my many homegrown ones is, "So you bought a book about playing dominoes and now you're going to Longworth and win? Yeah, right. I think you're fixing to pay a lot of dues." A real life one of these, no analogies, believe it or not, goes like this: Frances and I taught our youngest daughter Alison and her husband how to play forty-two. They could hardly wait to go back to see his folks so they could play the game with Nana and Papaw and clean their plow. That's been quite awhile and we can't get them to talk about it yet.

Anyhow, Frances and I went to Oklahoma to see Alison and Jamey, and a while after we crossed the river we came to the first of three toll-road booths. You know, the ones where you drive up to a red light and throw a handful of quarters over into a metal deal that looks like a planter box on a 12 Farmall planter. Then you wait for the light to turn from red to green, and off you go.

Well, sixteen quarters later when we were through all the tollbooths, I got to thinking on it and decided that I don't think you can beat that kind of a deal. Imagine, you're sitting in a booth listening to the radio or reading a book and here comes somebody driving seventy-five miles per hour who stops, throws money into a hopper and then takes off like something is after him. It appears that this goes on all the time, one car right after the other, on, on and on and on. It takes us thirty-two quarters to go see the kids and come home, and judging by the traffic it looks like a lot of folks must have kids up there beyond the toll road.

Naturally, I got to thinking about having my own toll road at Palava. Just think of all the people that live out there, maybe a half dozen or so, and all the oilfield traffic, maybe a couple a day. The postman comes six days a week, and if you throw in the road hunters it all might add up to ten or twelve vehicles per day. Of course, you would have to allow for a few off days. I told Frances I went to the farm (it's not on the expressway) the other morning and the road had been graded. I went in through a pasture gate at 7:45, sprayed sprouts all day and came out at 7:00 that night to find that no one had crossed my tracks. This is a sign that points to my having to run the tollbooth myself and maybe charging quite a bit for each vehicle.

While we were in Oklahoma, I showed Frances a highway sign and told her the Oklahoma jokes might not be exaggerated. The sign read Access Road, and I said, "Look, they don't even know how to spell 'excess', ha ha."

....

P.S. Overheard a great big ole boy at the Dairy Queen talking on a cellularized telephone saying, "Yeah, that salesman said he could put me in a '06 Dodge..." And I couldn't help wondering, "How big is that salesman anyway?"

Waking Up

SOME PEOPLE JUST naturally wake up in the morning without even setting an alarm. Y'reckon? Yeah, they do. I know, because I'm one of them. I don't ever set the alarm, because I won't sleep any later without waking up anyway. Some people set alarm clocks or radios or televisions to come on at a certain time. A time-setting coffee maker is another way to get them up.

I don't ever have to worry about sleeping too long, because something in the neighborhood will always wake me. It may be the dumpster truck or a diesel pickup. I usually get up at 5:30, but just in case I don't, I have Otis Lee. He's a Beagle puppy I got for my birthday. He has to sleep in this cage-type affair to keep him from running around the yard during the night barking. Maggie Mae, his big sister Jackrat, can take care of any necessary barking. I usually put Otis in his "room" at night along about dark. The other night I wanted to go to bed early, so I put him to bed early---I found out that won't work. The next morning, when he'd been in bed the usual number of hours, he decided it was high time I let him out and fed him. It was 5:10. So, since Otis had slept enough I guess I had, too. He just whines at first, but is on the way to getting loud if I don't get there pretty soon. He can start sounding like a big hound dog pretty quick. The book says he's an English Rabbit Hound, but I guess he'll have to chase cottontails and jackrabbits around here. We're a bit short on English rabbits! I took Maggie Mae and Otis Lee with me this morning and let them play about three hours while I was hoeing sunflowers out of a feed patch, so I think they'll sleep soundly enough tonight.

Normally I like to wake up easy and lie there two or three minutes trying to remember such things as who I am, and where I might be, and on to what time of year it is, and what day. After fourteen years in the welding business of jumping up and running right after the phone rang at any time of the night, I was ready for a change. Now I can wake up and get up any time during the night, and I can also go back to sleep easily. If I've just gone to bed and have been asleep thirty minutes or so, the girls will tell you that I may not be coherent if I have to answer the phone. A lot of people tell me they use the time to figure things out or solve problems when they wake up during the night.

Once in a while, after I think I've had an unusually trying day and didn't get enough sleep that night, I may get up the next morning and tell Frances, "I'm going to bed tonight at ten till seven." Of course she wants to know why I've picked such a strange bedtime, so I tell her, "Well, right now it just sounds like a real good time."

....

P.S. Overheard a woman in the bank say she was going home after work and cook enough butter beans for a camp meeting.

174

Dragging Things Out

I REMEMBER GOING visiting with Mama when I was a kid. Sometimes we might go by to see somebody that had a boy about my age, and we could play awhile. You can imagine, we thought we had at least all day. Y'reckon? Yeah, we did, even though Mama would probably say, "Now don't y'all start dragging out a bunch of stuff because we have to go pretty soon." Of course we wouldn't listen—we'd set in to getting out all the toys in the closet anyway, or going outside to get a pretty good start on building a hideout. If things were the other way around and company had come to our house, we might start off down to the tank to go swimming or start planning to ride the horses. Either way, about the time we were just about to start the real part of our playing we'd hear, "Come on, we have to go now and get home!" Which would bring on, "Oh Mama! We were just barely getting started." And then Mama would say, "I told you we couldn't stay long."

As is often the case, some things in our adult lives are a grownup version of waiting till we've got all the toys out and everything ready before we can begin to play. What is it now that's the same thing? We're always waiting for something—waiting till the kids get to a certain place in their lives or accomplish whatever they're trying to. Waiting till a parent gets settled in a new or different place. We may be waiting until we get something paid off, or waiting on results from a medical test. Or it may be something like thinking we'll take a trip as soon as all the wheat is planted or the cows are moved.

Sometimes things get really involved and handed down the line like a relay, with more and more people involved. Maybe you're waiting on John and Mary to do something, but they can't do whatever it is until Bob and Suzie do a different thing. Just about the time you're ready to give up on the whole thing, Bob and Suzie really do come through, and that's the first link in the chain. Then, don't you know, John and Mary won't get around to doing what they were supposed to do to make the second link in the chain, or, worse yet, they come up with a list of excuses of why they're not ever going to do it after all. And all the while your hand-cranked ice cream is melting in the freezer.

Scenarios like these can go on and on, from the time we're just kids until we're way past grown up and we discover that we spent all our time waiting and getting ready to play, and that a lot of the playing never got done at all. And then, one day right out of the blue and very unexpectedly, we'll hear a voice with the ultimate authority say, "It's time to go home now."

....

P.S. It's shocking how our minds adjust to accept things that we really don't like. As I pulled up to the gas pump yesterday, I was expecting to see that gas had gone up quite a bit since last Monday. The posted price was $2.49.9 and I thought, "Oh good, it's only $2.49.9--SAY WHAT???!!

Starting Over or Stopping

ONCE IN A great while, or maybe not so great a while, something gets to be such a mess that you may just have to start over! Y'Reckon? Yeah, I do. Matter of certain fact, I noticed one such thing this week. I drove up to the front of the Post Office and started to park, but the only available parking place would have caused me to park astraddle of a line. I backed up and moved down three places and found the same thing, so I parked anyway. This was during Post Office prime time--9:30-10:00 a.m.--so what could I do about it? One person had started this and it wasn't me (sounds like a second grader, doesn't it?) But whoever or whenever, it was probably going to go on until the middle of the afternoon, or it might not even start over in the right order until the next morning. All of this is not a big deal at all, nothing to worry about. But so many times something is a big deal and no one knows where it started or even why. And really, when you think about it, even if you knew who started it, what could be done about it now? We'd have somebody to blame it on, but that wouldn't fix it, so why bother?

What's the big outstanding thing right now that's been started and goes on and on and on and becomes more horrible by the day? The War. I don't know if we need it, I don't know if we don't, I don't know if it will ever accomplish anything. I don't know if it won't. That's all I keep saying. I don't know. I do know that the number of lives lost keeps growing every day. And we don't even know when, exactly where, or who will be next. But one thing we do know is that whoever it is will be not just a number but a human being. It will be an American citizen, someone's son or daughter, a spouse, a parent, a sibling, a close family member, a distant family member, a loved one, a neighbor, an old college roommate or school friend or maybe a mere acquaintance.

Let's think for a while about how this probably really is. A young couple finds out they are going to be parents. They're so excited. The day finally comes and they have the child, name it and bring it home. They take care of it and watch it learn to walk and play and finally start talking. Too soon, it's time to start to school, and they never will forget that first day of school. And then after twelve years and so much learning and playing and fun and problems, it's graduation time. This is after countless classes, books, parties, friends, tricycles, bicycles, cars, toys, sports equipment, pets, good times and troubled times. Maybe then it's on to college, or a job, or starting a career, or working with the family to take over the business or farm some day.

Or maybe all of a sudden, it's the military, with hours and hours of training. And too soon this son or daughter is halfway around the world in some place we can't even imagine. The parents and a whole lot of others are hoping, wishing and praying for his safe return. But no, one day comes word that he's gone, through, dead. Probably in an instant, or at least you hope it was. Then there's the hysteria, grief, anger, depression and at last emptiness and numbness. And then, forever, the why? Why? Why? That probably will never be answered. Little children will ask what happened to this parent, or relative, or friend. Someone tells them the truth and they ask, "Why?" Where do you go from there? Again, I'm saying, "I don't know." Maybe we need this war. Maybe it's necessary. I really and truly don't know. But I do know that Americans, loved ones, family members are dying, so I hope it is. One more thing I wonder, though. Remember the Viet Nam War? I wonder what we learned from all the lives, money and time lost in that one. Do you remember one of the chief sayings back then of the rebellious group that called themselves "hippies"? Oh, sure you do--"Suppose they gave a war and nobody came?"

. . . .

P.S. We got real tired of having beans and cornbread every night, so tonight we had cornbread and beans.

Credit Cards

MOST OF US could write a book of the door-stopper variety about the times telemarketers have called us with unbelievable credit-card deals that we absolutely could not live without a minute longer. Y'reckon? Yeah, or anyway I know I could. I just can't imagine how many credit cards must be out there and available, and I also can't figure out if they're having lots of luck with these calls selling the cards to people and keeping on keeping on, or if they aren't having any luck at all but are still trying. I do know if I'm eating dinner about 12:30 on Saturday and have to get up to answer what we call the "farm phone", the caller definitely will be a telemarketer. It's like they're looking in the window or something.

The farm phone has the number we had originally when we first got phones at Palava. Mama had it in town after she moved from the farm, and we eventually moved it to our house. Later on, the girls had that number for their phone. The problem now is that it rings in Alison's room and in the office, and we may or may not hear it. I tried to get the phone company not to list the number because our other number that we've had since 1971 is listed and rings all over the house, and we will hear it. Guess what I found out? It costs extra to leave a phone number out of the phone book! Say what? Do you know of anything else that you have to pay a monthly fee *not* to have? I thought protection insurance was just something the mob had in the northeast.

After about three years I finally did get our house phone number listed first before the farm phone. The problem now is that in the directory the farm phone also has the farm address. Why? I have no idea. There's no mailbox or anything out there. One day a poor UPS man called the farm phone number from the donut shop. He was tired and hungry and said he'd nearly run out of gas driving five miles up and down County Road 130 looking for a house to deliver to. Frances told him he was just a couple of blocks from our house on Woodruff right then. What was he trying to deliver? Talk about irony! It was a modem from the phone company itself!

Back to credit cards. Did you know the average per-cardholder-debt in the United States today is in excess of $8,562.00? That is really concerning. Credit card stories are falling out of the sky and coming from all directions. The stories are usually in the line of, "Well, they sent them young'uns a bunch of them ol' credit cards and now we're gonna hafta bail 'em out. It's gonna might nigh break us," or, "No, those people can't buy a car or house or anything else since they ruined their credit with charge cards." Some people have those holders that look like billfolds. When you see them you're afraid they're going to be full of grandkid pictures, but it turns out they're full of credit cards. By the way, I read a warning that said some thieves won't steal a whole billfold or card holder, but will take out just one card. By the time the owner misses the card it may be time for "slow walking and sad singing."

This country that we enjoy living in was not built on credit cards or unsecured debt. Somewhere down the road or over the hill there has to be a day of reckoning or a big balancing out. And now we have people who get on television and tell you if you'll come see them you may not have to pay for all that ol' stuff you bought and charged but don't want anymore. After all, they more or less insinuate that somebody made you buy all that stuff that now is so "last week". I find it amusing to envision the scene if the credit card debtors won't even pay the man who is saving them from themselves. I don't think I would have a warm fuzzy secure feeling being employed by a bunch of people in trouble because they hadn't paid their debts.

....

P.S. Economics Professor Green from Georgia Tech wrote a syndicated column titled, "There's No Such Thing as an Unpaid Debt---Someone Has to Pay It."

Stuff and More Stuff to Do

"FOLLOW ME," HE said, and Matthew got up and followed Him. Y'reckon? Yeah, I do, because that's what it says in the second part of Matthew 9:9. As I was reading this, I got to going around town and the neighborhood in my mind trying to think of anybody today who would do as Matthew did---just get up and walk away from everything and follow Jesus. Guess what? I didn't really ever find anyone. Later we'll talk about what type of person it would be who would do that now, okay?

One reason we couldn't find anyone to do as Matthew did is because we have so much stuff to stay and see about or take with us. All of this stuff we have just keeps coming back on my screen. We have stuff we've bought, stuff we've been given for gifts or that someone else was tired of having. We have stuff we've had for so long we don't even know where it came from, but somehow we don't want to get rid of it. And lots of times if we do let it go, it's just so we can make room for more stuff. There's so much that we can't find the stuff we want or maybe even need. Every weekend it seems like there are garage sales and yard sales all around, with people getting rid of stuff they don't need, want or care about anymore. And what is all this stuff, anyway? Insecurities? Insulation? Some of it may tie us back to an earlier time; some of it is a status symbol. Some of it is for convenience, or we may actually even need it.

And now, to do before we follow anyone. Oh, my! Where do we even start? Can't you just hear it? "I'll have to call such and such." "I have to e-mail so and so," or, "I have to check my e-mail." "I have to pay a bill and mail it." "But, but I have an appointment tomorrow that took forever to get." "But I told them I'd meet them tomorrow, and . . ." Maybe we should stop and think and question why we insist on being so busy. What are we hiding from? What are we insulating ourselves against?

Why don't we stop and smell the flowers? What are we in such a hurry about, and why? We've seen on television how things can change in a very short time. How much stuff did the victims of Katrina and Rita have left? How many so-important things did they all of a sudden leave undone? I mean, they were de-stuffed in a short period of time, and their appointment books, phones, and computers were gone, too. Don't you imagine that some of them would like to point out to us how silly we've become, and how far we've strayed from real life as it should be?

Sometimes I play a mental game where I imagine having a box I can take around the house and put whatever I want to keep in it. That's all, I mean all, I can have. The box? Oh, it's about the size that would hold packages of paper towels. Study on that awhile. Then think that when some of our parents were young that box would've held all they owned and had room left over.

Oh, yeah! The person who would follow? I imagine someone who we'd call a "free spirit", or even a hippie. A person we might have thought didn't have many values. Y'reckon?

• •

P. S. Sit on a stump and watch the ants crawl around while you study on this: I'm afraid we've evolved to the point of falsely assuming that the more stuff we have and the bigger hurry we're in, the more important we are.

P'rade

TODAY IS JULY the Fourth, 2006. It's the 230th birthday of our Declaration of Independence. Wonderful, absolutely wonderful! Y'reckon? Yeah, it is. Today Frances and I were going to feed cattle (in July? Yeah, it's really sad, and dry, too) and she was telling me that Thomas Jefferson was thirty-three years old when he wrote the Declaration. I guess we picture him being this wise old grayhead that was a bit tottery, but thirty-three?

Today is also the 125th anniversary of Nolan County (Fisher County, too---rah, rah!) Just imagine. The few folks that were here then lived in tents or dugouts or half-dugouts. The first residents to settle and build such shelters in the Eskota area told of a man who was there when they arrived. They said he just lived out on the prairie. Records show that the first Anglo child was born in the southeast corner of Nolan County in 1876. His name was Tony Medley, and, as it turns out, he was the grandfather of Bill Medley. (Oh, sure you do---he's half of the Righteous Brothers who recorded "You've Lost That Loving Feeling"!) The few and scattered residents hereabouts were still constantly concerned about raids by unchecked nomadic warlike Native Americans. The last recorded such raid was in Bird Nest Canyon. The railroad came along during those early times and brought passenger trains and freight trains and all that came with them. It also started the sale of lots in Original Town, Sweetwater. The first lot sold was where Azteca is now, to a man named J. S. Johnson---it didn't say whether his name was Jack Stanley.

Of course, also in early times Spanish explorers left inscriptions east of Sweetwater Creek along about the middle of the county. And then, in the middle 1850's, when Robert Edward Lee and his troop of soldiers were up around what is now Rotan on patrol, they found Indian signs and horse tracks but not much else. In a letter, Robert Edward told his wife that the area was "infested with prairie dogs and rattlesnakes," and was probably of no use for anything except maybe a penal colony. If he could see all of the prisons scattered around now, would he claim to have had that much foresight?

"P'rade"? Oh, yeah. I rode Holly's horse in the Fourth of July parade today. It was a lot of fun. Back when we rode and showed horses a lot, a deal like today was simple---saddle a horse, jump him into the trailer, and go. But now, it's like go to the farm, bring a horse in, ride him around the pasture two different times. Stand him in a muddy pen corner nearly all day so his feet can be trimmed, comb his mane and tail. Clean up a saddle. Feed the horse about daylight, then go back and get a trailer. Saddle and load the horse, and go get in line for the "p'rade".

The parade was loads of fun with lots of horses---eighteen of them, lots of old cars and floats and plenty of spectators. And the band concert following it was wonderful, with a nice ceremony and Lou Ann Pyburn's vocal talent. Being a music person from way back, I can tell you if you don't know that we're very fortunate to have such a high-quality band here in our town. And the best part is that all these talented people are ours---as in, they belong here!

The Lions Club was responsible for the celebration, and there were a lot of good ol' patriotic people to enjoy it. Some of them were new to our area (yea!) and some of them can point and show you where their great granddaddy lived and maybe even where his chicken house was. Brenda Kay from the Sweetwater Reporter, along with her spouse Warren Lynn from the Chamber of Commerce, worked really hard on all these festivities, including Sunday night's first-class fireworks display. I told Brenda Kay how great it all was, and of course she's never out of additional ideas. Her response was, "I think next year we should have ice cream, don't you?" I think maybe she meant hand-cranked ice cream---y'reckon?

．．

P.S. Lisa Peterson brought along one of her dogs, and so did some other people. It's always nice to have the dogs. I just hope Maggie Mae and Otis Lee don't hear about it.

No Problem! No Problem?

SOME OF THE things that kids (young folks) say these days are really puzzling to me. Y'reckon? Yeah, as a matter of certain fact they are. I know by the manner of these kids that they're meaning to be pleasant and helpful, but I can't imagine that they know how they sound to us old fogies who have been used to other terms. For instance, the other day I went into this place and got a whole bunch of stuff and as the clerk was adding it up I was looking in my checkbook and doubting that the balance was going to exceed the total of all I had bought. I wrote the check, tore it out, and handed it to the store owner, and then I turned around and started out. When I got nearly to the door without anybody saying a word to me I thought, "Okay, I'll try this." So before I left I turned around and said, "Thank you!" I guess I was thinking, "Thank you for allowing me to spend all my money here." And what response did I get? "No problem!" I mean, that is what was said. "No problem!" I just went on out thinking, "I'm glad to know it wasn't a problem for me to buy all this stuff from you." Surely these people don't have any idea how they sound. I've tried to figure out where or why on earth all this started. Many times these annoying and worn-out expressions started with some television advertising or sit-com. If you know about this one, please tell me!

I think back on things that caught on over the years and were used to apply or vaguely apply to all sorts of situations—"The Shadow knows." Sergeant Preston saying, "On, King!" Rowdy Yates on Rawhide saying, "Head 'em up! Move 'em out!" Chester on Gunsmoke saying,

"Mr. Dillon, Mr. Dillon!" The best one we used to use was from a commercial with the guy in the super efficiency apartment where the medicine cabinet could be opened from two apartments. This sleepy guy opens his side up at the same time an over-zealous morning type opens the other side with a cheery, "Hi, guy!" He continues with a long spiel, and finally Sleepy Guy looks back over his shoulder and calls out helplessly, "Mona," trying to call his wife to save him. So whenever someone had us treed we'd try to look helpless and say, "Mona!" It really was a hoot. (Well, maybe you had to be there.) Of course, my all-time hang-on-forever favorite was from the movie *Cool Hand Luke* with Paul Newman, where the prison warden played by Strother Martin (talk about one of a kind!) was telling his chain gang after an incident with Cool Hand Luke, "What we have here is a failure to communicate." Then there was the not very good one to start with, but a real hanger-on, "Where's the beef?" Another one that's more recent but pretty much gone now is the "Whazzz Up?" That one was pretty good and I really didn't think it would wear off. One of the best all-time ones to me was during the time of the Teenage Mutant Ninja Turtles when Michaelangelo said, "Pizza Dude's got thirty seconds, Man."

Back to the puzzling things of late. Frances and I were eating Mexican food in a nice place the other night and the waitress, a nice young lady, asked, "Would you like sopaipillas?" We said we would, so she said, "Okay, let me go grab a couple of them." Grab? Grab? Where in the world did that come from? Grab is what you do when a young'un or a puppy is fixing to jump out the window of a pickup when you're driving. Or more like, "Okay, you take the broom and get on the other side of the bed and poke it under there and when Fluffy runs out I'll grab her." I couldn't help thinking, "Oh, please don't grab the sopaipillas! They might not even be fit to eat when you get here with them!" It just puzzles me as to how that ever caught on.

This, That and Some More

SOMETIMES I GET the urge to write a cleanup story about things that are important but won't make a whole article in themselves. Y'reckon? Yeah, I do. You know what I mean---it's kinda like every now and then you don't plow all day or whatever, you just have a cleanup or catch-up day for loose ends. You might go feed, go by the cleaners, post office, bank and feed store and then tighten the screws in the den doorknob before it falls plumb off. That's what I'm doing here.

I started to write a letter to the editor of the Abilene Reporter-News, but, hey y'all! This is my paper and our paper, so this is where it needs to be. The front page of the Abilene Reporter-News last Wednesday morning showed a giant backhoe-type machine with a claw bucket on it tearing down a house! I thought about the Sour Sites our paper ran for awhile, and I was going to say, "Sour Sites? Sour Sites? How about sad sights!" Look at the house they're demolishing! It could have been in the north center part of our town. I know a lot of people who live in houses that don't look nearly that good and some more people who don't even have a house. And here they're spending money to tear houses down and haul them to a growing dump ground so they can spend 149 million to build some more. Say what? I've said this before, but some of us will live to see the United States of America punished for her waste. In our town there's presently a movement called Habitat for Humanity that is trying to get started improving properties to make them livable. Just think how much better that is.

Well, it snowed again. 'Member, I said if the snow stayed on the ground three days it would snow again? I wonder if this one will stay three days. And this is Groundhog Day. I don't have a groundhog, but my saddle horses came out of the barn this morning and didn't see their shadows. A fellow told me the other day he doesn't make any new year's resolutions during the hype and such but always waits till Groundhog Day. Sounded pretty country to me. And you know, if it sounds pretty country to me, well guess what?

I read on the front of the paper this morning about a group assigned to study global warming that has decided it is "very likely caused by humans." I imagine most of you would say, "Who, me? What did I do?" I must admit I really don't know, nor do they. Lots of things are hard for me to imagine, but I do realize that in some places they have as many folks as we have horses, cattle, chickens, goats and stalks of cotton. It makes me glad I'm here. The report was twenty pages long, which causes me to wonder about it in itself. Maybe the amount of winter we've gone through this year will change some of the theories that our whole weather pattern has changed.

· ·

P.S. After I finally got the ice maker going Frances was going to throw away all our old ice trays until I reminded her how handy they'd be to feed her chickens out of.

It's Always Something

I'VE JUST BEEN thinking and noticing things. Y'reckon? Yeah, I have. Last week I said something about global warming. Well, that started me to thinking about all the talk, reports, books and charts that are out now about that subject. It seems like it's what's "in" now. What will it be next? I don't know but I can assure you it will be something because it seems like we always have to have some kind of hurrahing, constantly causing some sort of cloud or impending dread. Allow me to "example you", as the old folks say.

I remember when I was little some folks rightfully lived in real dread and worry that we'd have another Great Depression and it would start next week. At least that was (and is) something that could happen and had in fact just recently ended. Then there was the concern that the Russians were going to fly directly over Palava and drop a big bomb. We had to salute the flag while we still could before the Russians took it down and made slaves out of all of us. I'm serious. I lived through it.

Then we were all going to be blown away by a tornado. We had to spend a lot of time in the scare hole (cellar) hoping the house didn't blow over on the door leaving us down there to starve. Of course there wouldn't be any neighbors to rescue us because the ones the Russians hadn't already got were blown plumb out of Fisher County since they didn't have a storm cellar. I remember one of Daddy's cousins saying every time it came up a cloud we'd all run to the storm cellar just like a bunch of prairie dogs going down a hole.

Well, after we survived this we had a UFO scare and it got really bad. Folks were seeing them all over everywhere, some even flying in formation. There was speculation that they could probably see down in a storm cellar or anywhere else. Then we had the Cuban Missile Crisis, and the only thing to do after that was have a fallout shelter built and stock it with enough food and water to last forever, nearly.

Awhile later things got into such an unbelievable mess that the only thing with a ghost of a chance of saving a handful of us was transcendental meditation, or TM, as it was popularly known. Following that, we had one that came right out of the blue and was going to end it all. It was called "The Population Explosion". Before long there would be so many people we'd be standing on top of each other. All the whole Big Bend area of Texas would be so crowded it would probably look like Singapore.

And then came the shortage scare. There was a shortage of everything you can imagine. Before it was over there was even a shortage of notepads to write down what there were shortages of, or pencils to write with. I think the latest big one broke all records, though. Books, articles, speeches, newscasts and more warned us about the all time prize-winning Y2K. May we be delivered, please! I saw people with great loads of water, canned goods, Coleman stoves and fuel, batteries, flashlights, guns and shells, and no telling what all else. Others got all upset with each other when talking turned to arguing. One day in a real estate class I set my bucket down and said, in an effort to resolve the arguments, "We don't know what day, month or year it is anyway." That didn't work---I thought I would be stoned! My second futile attempt to pacify everyone failed, too. I just said a Julian calendar was used until 1582 when Pope Gregory VIII introduced the Gregorian calendar, which Great Britain and our colonies adopted in 1752. I was in luck, though. Soon after that day *Time* Magazine printed a long article about calendars and how there were so many, and they had been changed back and forth, and one time centuries ago a king even made a calendar change of more than two hundred days. So! Hello, y'all. We don't know. We do know when the Vernal and Autumnal equinoxes are just by equal amounts of light and dark. We do know when the moon is full and how long it is from sunrise to sunrise and from sunup to sundown. But what else do we really know? Of course a lot of this scare had to do with computers not being programmed to change, but there were many more buggers to find, some with religious overtones. So, in conclusion, I maintain that we don't know where we are in time right now, but does it really matter?

....

P. S. I'm going to bed now but I plan on getting up early tomorrow morning to see if the sun rises or if it has already burned up.

Memory Triggers

IT'S FUNNY HOW you can see, hear or smell something that triggers a nearly-forgotten memory. It can happen when you're on a mission, in a hurry or whatever, and all of a sudden, wham! There it is. Y'reckon? Yeah, I do. The other morning before I was ready to leave the house for the day I decided to hurry to Brookshire's for a few things to add to breakfast. In the store I rounded a corner in a fast walk and suddenly stopped when I saw a display of school supplies with an array of colored paper, notebooks and other things. I thought, "Oh my, it was so exciting to start to school." I remembered how it was with all the planning, anticipation and apprehension about a totally new adventure. When I started first grade I never had been around a school except the one at Palava. It had closed after the first six weeks in the fall of 1943, so I don't remember children and classes being taught there, but I do remember going to Halloween parties and plays.

My first-grade class started to school in the basement of the First Methodist Church, since the northeast wing was being built onto East Ward and was not completed in time. There was no lunchroom, so we had to take our own lunches from home. Mine was usually a pimiento cheese sandwich wrapped in waxed paper. Tin foil was in short supply since we were barely out of World War II. (I could have said after the war, but some of the real young set might have thought I meant the Civil War.) There was no such thing then as Baggies or Ziplocs. My lunch pail had a thermos that probably held a cup of milk with a cork stopper and cup lid. School was so exciting and so much fun, and we had recess and lunch and all kinds of paper, glue, scissors and Crayolas. The first thing every morning we'd line up on the church steps, with a separate line for each teacher's class. We had yellow pencils and Big Chief tablets. I remember being in line with Patricia Holladay, Jean Pace, Bettye Boothe, Carolyn Bruner, Ardis D. Gaither, Carl Cowan, Jackie Choate, Roy Wayne Caldwell and W. Lee Rawlings.

The church was a couple of blocks north of the railroad tracks. One morning we came to school and found out they'd "blown the train out" the night before. I didn't and still don't know what that consisted of, but the result was soot all over everything. Some of the town kids got to school early and played on the school steps and around in the soot and were a total mess and covered with it. It was awful and the teachers were all upset and trying to clean up the sooty kids. (Oh, no, you didn't call little Tommy's mother to come get him. There might not even have been a phone in that building for all I know. And Tommy's mother might not have had a phone anyway.)

I well remember the first time I got "told on" at school and was sooo embarrassed. We were learning how to make our 1's, 2's, 3's and so on, and I guess when Mrs. Jones showed us how to make an 8 I wasn't paying any attention. (That must have been the first of about a jillion times that has happened.) Anyway, I looked up on the blackboard and there was an 8. Now 8's are a big step for little cowboys with new pencils, so I thought, "Oh, well, I can get there somehow (also the first of about a jillion times), so I drew a zero and then drew another zero on top of that one. It looked good to me, but W. Lee saw me do it and went through the full scale of pointing and saying, "Ummm, ummm", before he raised his hand and said to Mrs. Jones, "Stanley don't know how to make a 8." Oh! Oh! To die and crawl in a hole! Every kid in there turned around and looked at me. (I still make an eight like that sometimes, but I sure wouldn't let W. Lee see me!)

••

P. S. Today I saw Carolyn Bruner in the tax office and we were talking about starting to school in the church basement (she had a different teacher) and later moving on to East Ward.

Eddie Mitchell was standing there listening to us and asked "Where was East Ward?" Carolyn looked at him like he'd asked where the post office was, so I told him, "That's what we called Philip Nolan."

Progress?

MORE AND MORE all the time we hear about progress here and there and how "progressive" things are. Y'reckon? Yeah, I do, but sometimes it seems like the progress turns out to be like a one-on-one game where one person wins and it's great---right? But wait, now. That means another person has to lose, and that's not so great. For instance, years ago Sweetwater's school enrollment increased dramatically. "Great!" you say. Well, maybe so, maybe no. Great for Sweetwater, yes. But the increase came as a result of the consolidation of several smaller schools, and that signaled the end for communities like Busby, Eskota, Longworth and Palava. They immediately started downhill and didn't stop until they hit the bottom. Then they became just a memory that people tried for awhile to keep alive, but that has definitely faded away. For instance, who among us could now name the schools that closed and consolidated with Palava or Eskota? See?

I see houses now in Sweetwater that used to be neighborhood grocery stores. The stores closed, and their customers went to shop at one of the five or six big grocery stores we had here in the Sixties and Seventies. In 1980, if my headlights had been brighter than my taillights and I had written that we would have just one grocery store twenty-five years from then in 2005, you would have thought I'd been out in the country too long. (Save all this on your screen, because it is going somewhere, really.) What if in 1970 I had said that so many of the businesses we had then wouldn't be here now and that even our

198

hospital would be closed and torn down and a new one built out close to Interstate 20?

I remember a short thirty years ago or so, we had three meat-packing houses in Sweetwater. The people doing business with them and working there probably thought business and working conditions would be the same forever. Now there are four packing houses serving the United States. Let's review this: There were almost as many packing houses in Sweetwater as there are now in the whole nation. We used to have car lots, automotive, tractor and boat dealerships all over town. We had more churches and filling stations here than nearly anywhere else I can remember. How many filling stations do we have now? How many small or country churches have closed? How many churches that used to be quite large are struggling to keep going now? All of this "progress" seems like big car dealers are being bought out by bigger car dealers, big stores are gobbling up small stores, and big banks are taking over smaller banks. It was on the news the other day that Wal-Mart makes 20,998 dollars a minute or 36 million dollars an hour. And now they're trying to put banks in their stores.

Let's turn on our bright headlights and fast forward to this: All towns in Texas are suburbs of Dallas, Houston, San Antonio, Austin, El Paso or Amarillo. They all have mega schools, hospitals and Wal-Marts. You can go to a Wal-Mart that has a bank inside it, a huge automobile dealership across the street with a hospital beside it, and, if it's the right time of the week, you can go to the drive-in church on the way home.

Those That Have Passed

Adrian Edward Mullican, Jr.

ONCE IN A while there's a funny timing to things that happen. Y'reckon? Yeah, there is. Let me tell you about the most recent and jarring one. The other day at the office, Brenda Scott and I were reviewing the old oilfield boom days. I just happened, for some reason unknown to me now, to ask her, "Do you know Punk Mullican?" She said, "No, not personally." I went on to tell her that Punk was the most accommodating man I had ever known. I told her stories of how I had a welding shop at 207 Ash Street and Punk had a diesel mechanic shop right across the street. We used to "neighbor" a lot, as we in the country say. I can remember him coming over and saying he had something cut, cleaned up and ground off, and if I'd just back a truck across the street he would hold up whatever it was while I welded it on. And then when it was real cold and we'd have a welder, truck or winch truck that didn't want to start, here Punk would come across the street and get it started.

I remember one day Punk had a truck and trailer parked in the street on his side and I had a pulling unit parked in the street on my side. We were trying to work on and around them, and the people driving up and down the street were not happy with us. This was not unusual at all. We'd always laugh and say maybe the City would build a bridge from Broadway to Third Street and we could work under it in the shade while the traffic went over us. I told Brenda some of these real-life adventures, and then the very next night Frances was reading the paper and exclaimed, "Oh, no! Punk died!" I was completely astounded.

At the funeral, there were cars and pickups parked all around everywhere. So many people. Punk's daughters-in-law spoke at the service, Keith Clifton was the preacher, and it was all so good. During it all, I reviewed times we had together. Lots of times--day times, night times, horribly hot times, unbelievably cold times, but mostly good times.

I remembered one time asking Punk where his nickname had come from, and he said, "Oh, back at home folks called me and Mama 'Punk and Pokey'." I came to learn that was not an unusual answer for him. I told him it was pretty common for me to rename folks I was around a lot. This was in the early 70's and one of the "in" words was super. So I called Punk "Super Mechanic", which soon became just "Super M". He liked that, and called me "Super Welder".

Things changed, as they often do, and Super M became the shop foreman at a great big truck stop. You guessed it—there's not one of the 168 hours in a week that I haven't been to that truck stop with a welding truck. The phone would ring at 2:30 a.m. and I'd hear Super M say, "Super Welder, this ole boy thought we were going to have to get a part from Abilene in the morning, but I told him you could weld it and we could get him going tonight." And I don't know of the times he would show up late at his shop or wherever and say, "Oh, I had to help this guy that was having trouble with his pickup." I'd ask, "Who was it?" To which he would answer, "I don't know, but he seemed like a good ole boy."

I remember when Punk's sons Jeff and Daryl thought it was high time he got caught up with the times, as kids are prone to do. They pooled their money and bought him a calculator. Guess what? He still added up unbelievably long columns of figures in his head, and they were right!

People who work seven twenty-fours like to tell stories about getting up in the middle of the night to go on a job. Super M always won when he told about getting up in the night and jerking on a boot and then discovering one of his boys had put a hand full of marbles in it! Oh, ouch!

Lately we hear all kinds of phrases used like, "He passed, he crossed over, he went to his maker, he went to heaven." I don't know which one of these Super M would have used, but I do know for a certain certified fact that he is there, and he's helping someone.

Leon

MOST MEN ARE somewhere in the great middle mass of humanity, but a few who demonstrate unusual traits manage to rise to the top of their world and environment. An old expression most of us have heard, "He rides a tall, fast horse and swings a wide loop," always brings to my mind an image of Leon Goswick. Y'reckon? Yeah, I do. It's kinda funny in a way, since in all the thirty-two years I knew Leon I don't remember ever seeing him horseback. Once in a Gunsmoke scene Matt rode up to this homestead-looking place where a woman was outside boiling and punching down clothes in a black wash pot. Matt spoke to her and asked where her husband was because he needed to talk to him. The woman said, "He's up the creek a ways." Matt said, "I've been told he's an unusual man." The woman said, "Yeah, he's got his ways . . . but they're all his'n." I always thought that line fit Leon.

Frances and I had both been teaching in Odessa when we moved back to Sweetwater in July of 1971. She kept on teaching and I started welding. I heard of Leon around the oilfield but never did meet him until one Sunday at the Fourth and Elm Church in about 1975. I tried a couple of times to pass the time of day with him and he was cordial enough, but never would really thaw out, so I left him alone. Then one Sunday after dinner he called and said he had a cow with her back legs down in a cattle guard and he couldn't get her out. He asked if I could send him a welder. I told him one of my boys was gone to a drilling rig in my truck but I'd go get another truck and come out myself. I went to a place between Palava and Eskota and backed up to a cattle guard. I cut a pipe out of the cattle guard and Leon and I got the cow out. Then I welded the pipe back in and told him if he had a trailer nearby I'd take a come-along and we could get her in the trailer. He said no, he'd just bring water and feed to her. I'd already rolled up my leads and hose, so I started to leave and he said, "Much obliged—send me a bill."

Later on, in 1976, Leon made a deal with me to build some pens on that place and said he'd call a couple of days before he was ready. He called on Friday and said he'd be ready on Monday. He asked who was going to do it, and since my boys were on jobs already I said, "I am," and asked, "Who's going to help me?" He said, "I am." I worked out there eleven days. I don't know how to describe it. I guess I could point out that I was used to working long and hard and a lot, and by the weight chart I needed to gain eight pounds. I lost seven pounds. Leon was the best helper I ever had, but he was the boss, too. He'd forget to eat dinner—one day it was nearly two o'clock before he took time for it. He and a hand had already poured the post in concrete and it was kind of a mess, but I don't think it had taken long to do it. I asked Leon to bring a chain and boomer off the back of my truck. The top pipe rail was about six inches off the top of the post and four inches over. When Leon saw what I needed he dropped the chain and boomer, took the post in one hand and rail in the other, put them together, and said, "Weld it." While I was welding it (a tack wouldn't have held it) I thought, "Good Lord! *No one* is strong enough to do that!" But Leon did. We would always go to a little rock house down on the place and eat dinner (not necessarily at 12:00) and when we got through I'd think, "My Lord! *No one* can eat that much!" But Leon did. One time I sent Jeff Mullican to help Leon finish the inside of a barn. Marceline would bring Leon's lunch and some extra stuff for Jeff to add to his lunch. Jeff said the first day she showed up with the lunch he thought a bunch more folks were coming. He was pretty well spoiled when I got him back.

After the pens, Leon and I became good friends. We talked about everything from the lack of rain (it was March of 1976) to the world economy to local politics. I learned a lot from Leon, and I still remember it all and I'm seeing it come true. In all of our talking then and over the years I never heard him say anything bad about anyone, and words can't convey how much respect I have for that.

One Sunday after church Leon asked if he could use my winch truck, so I went down and let him in my shop yard. Marceline brought him to the shop, and he got out as I was going in to get the keys to Armbruster, my winch truck. When I came out he was checking the oil and water and kicking the tires. I thought that was really good, and realized not many people would do that. He said he was going to lift up a cattle guard, clean out from under it, and set it back down after dinner that day and would have my truck back in the morning. (Let me explain, for those of you who don't know. Leon and Marceline were going to go to church every Sunday and then that afternoon he was going to do more work than most people that thought they worked had done all week. Oftentimes it was with the help of Marceline.) My truck was at the gate when I got there Monday morning. Leon called that morning and asked how much he owed me and I told him not anything. He mailed me a check for fifty dollars. I would have done it myself for fifty dollars!

When I needed to borrow money back then, I would call Leon at night, since we were both gone all day. He'd say, "I'll be at the bank about 7:00 in the morning. Just come around and kick on that south door and I'll let you in." One time when some of us were talking about banking I told that story and the guy I was talking to said, "Wasn't he afraid to let somebody in at 7:00 in the morning when he was there by himself?" I said, "Apparently you didn't understand that I was talking about Leon."

Sometimes Leon would call and say he was going to a big cow sale or to look at a tractor or whatever and did I want to go? I'd tell him I did and he'd ask if it was all right if we left kind of early. I'd say, "Fine with me," and he'd say, "Okay, I'll pick you up about 4:30." We'd always stop and eat dinner somewhere. I can guarantee you it wouldn't be a place where they brought you a cup of soup and half a sandwich!

I like to read what I call "people signs." I'm not always right, but I keep trying. Let me teach you one. Picture a man wearing real Levi's, a western shirt or work shirt, scuffed-up boots, and a big hat. He will also wear a belt, carry a bandanna and a pocket knife and have a billfold in his front pocket, shirt pocket, or in the pickup. That billfold may have more green money in it than you made last month. He'll be driving a full-grown pickup, probably dirty, with a grill guard, headache rack, tool box, spare tire, air tank, high-lift jack, shovel and more. Inside there will be a flashlight or maybe two, and extra batteries. You might think, "In case he gets home late." Well, possibly, but really it means he can't wait for the sun to come up so he can get started. One time I said something to Leon about his always getting started early and he said, "Oh, not really. I've got a brother that's gone from the house every morning before I even get up." Then he added, "But he really does have a lot to see about."

Sometimes Leon talked to me a lot. One time he talked a long time and then seemed embarrassed and said, "Stan, I don't know why I told you all that. I just thought somebody needed to know." I said, "It's fine, Leon. I've had so many people say the same thing to me. I guess that's the star I was born under, but your story is safe with me. I won't ever tell anyone." I haven't and I won't, but I won't ever forget it, either.

What I can tell in conclusion is that Leon, like so many born in those years, came up real hard. He left Ranger on a freight train when he was fourteen years old. He got off at Colorado City and found a place where he could sleep for fifty cents a night and another place where he could buy two big hamburgers for fifty cents. He started hoeing cotton and making two dollars a day, so he was ahead a dollar every day! Later he lived with a family that farmed and had cattle and sheep. The lady of the house was a teacher and taught him at night. During this time Leon had an attack of appendicitis and that farmer gave the doctor a cow to pay for the operation.

After Leon served time in the military, he came back to Snyder. He bought him a new 1949 Ford and went to work for Bum Gibbons, who had pulling units, lots of them. Leon told me that during the Snyder oil boom he climbed a derrick one clear night when he was babysitting a new well. He counted over a hundred rigs running that night. I think he said a hundred and thirty-four, but I'm not sure.

During that time he met and married Marceline Guelker. She had the same work and thrift values that he did. They lived in Snyder and later in Sweetwater. They raised two daughters who have the same work ethic as their parents, and the daughters in turn married two men that are of the same cloth, and on and on and on. After Leon had open-heart surgery, his sons-in-law and I helped feed his cattle for awhile. I helped them on Tuesday mornings and also helped pen, separate and load cattle. That's when I learned that if I needed to know which calf belonged on which cow, Marceline was the one who knew. And she was always right!

Leon got his first pulling unit in 1954 and later on added an oilfield supply store and transport trucks. He also had land and cattle and more land and more cattle, and through all of this Marceline was right by him working as hard as he did. They had a ranch and cattle and also a small house in town at Sierra Blanca, where they often went to take care of things. On the last day of the trip out there they'd wind all their work up that day and then drive all night so they could be back here in time to go to work the next morning! (To avoid being reminded, I'll say, "Okay, okay, so I worked all day and night and all the next day sometimes when I was welding, but it wasn't my choice, and drilling rigs do run twenty-four hours and seven days.")

The banner that flies above all that Leon and Marceline have accomplished, which is much, would say, "Hard Work and Thriftiness." Few people unanimously agree on anything, but I'd venture to say that all the people who knew Leon in any capacity would agree that there never was one like him, and there won't be another one.

•••

P.S. A real popular and amusing saying that has caught on lately is, "Git'er done!" From the first time I heard a comedian say that, I've wished I could walk up to him and say, "Hey, Slim, if you haven't worked with, for, or around Leon Goswick, you don't even have a clue to what that means."

LaVergne, TN USA
30 July 2010
191412LV00005B/15/P